Basic Maintenance for the Vintage South Bend® Lathe

Published by
ILION Industrial Services, LLC
Raleigh, NC

ISBN: 978-1671537613

Copyright © 2020 by ILION Industrial Services, LLC

Disclaimer: ILION Industrial Services, LLC is neither affiliated with South Bend Lathe Inc. nor its successors and makes no claims as such. Any information or product offered is done so in good faith in order to assist vintage machinery owners and is neither sanctioned by South Bend Lathe Inc. nor its successors as OEM information, parts or products. ILION Industrial Services, LLC makes no warranty and accepts no liability for injury, property damage or any other costs incurred and/or damages suffered (including direct, indirect or consequential damages, as well as loss of income or profits) as a result of the use of any information or product contained or referenced herein. By the purchase and/or use of the information or products referenced in this publication, the user expressly accepts these terms and conditions.

**Oil is cheap
  Bearings are not…**

**Run the Lathe Dry
  You'll regret it a lot…**

** apologies to restroom
poets everywhere*

Index:

Forward	3
South Bend Lathe History	5
Lathe Parts Identification	7
General Maintenance Summary	8
Safety	11
Cleaning the Lathe	12
Lubricating the Lathe	21
Basic Lathe Adjustments	37
Reference Material	65
Owner Resources	70

Forward

The original South Bend Lathe Company was in operation for almost 100 years, during which time many models and variations of their precision lathes were manufactured. The information contained in this maintenance guide applies to all common versions of the benchtop and floor standing lathes that were produced by SBL from the 1930's through the early 1980's. Some of the material in this manual was taken from old SBL publications, while other material comes from newer sources and direct experience with vintage lathe owners. This book was assembled in order to provide an accessible, consistent and easily referenced resource for the vintage SBL owner by compiling a considerable amount of maintenance information into one publication and then updating older practices to be relevant today. Having worked with a numerous SBL owners over the last 20 years, we realized that most new "home machinists" were asking the same questions on a continuing basis. Though some of the answers could be found on various websites, forums and on-line publications, one had to know the correct terminology and where to look, so it was clearly difficult for a new user to digest so much information and try to make use of it while attempting to get their lathe back into action. The general lack of consolidated maintenance information was the primary reason for us producing our first manual over 10 years ago: A Guide to Renovating the South Bend Lathe 9" Model ABC & 10k. Based on the response we got from the SBL owner's community we must have done something right since the 30,000th copy of that manual just shipped this past summer. We never considered that there were that many South Bends and various clones still in existence. We had fully expected that the demand for the manual would disappear over time, but it has not. Consequently, we are taking the next step in our quest to keep these fine machine tools alive and running.

Regrettably, we have found that the primary cause for old South Bend Lathes being scrapped or "parted out" is poor maintenance. Sadly, many of these lathes had made it all the way from WWII factories, through school shops and small businesses, only to fall victim to poor maintenance 75 years later in someone's basement because they ran the lathe without oil or proper adjustment. Such simple and mundane procedures as properly oiling & cleaning the lathe are no longer taught in many high school and community colleges because they no longer have a "shop class" where these basic introductory skills were always taught in the past. In the absence of practical "hands-on" experience, most of the information and context for its use is gradually being lost over time.

Basic maintenance is essential for any lathe to have a long service life and though South Bend Lathes were well designed and are inherently indestructible, the two things that will make scrap-iron out of a perfectly good lathe is "dirt" and "lack of lubrication". The use of the correct oil, properly applied to the lathe and kept clean will ensure that the lathe will remain healthy. It is normal for some oil to seep out of the bearings onto lathe surfaces and that oil will attract dirt. Over time that oil & dirt combination will become solidified crud which must be removed periodically. A lathe in normal use should be disassembled every 7-10 years to clean out the petrified oil, grease, grime and metal chips from the inner workings and to replace consumable items such as wicks, gaskets belts, etc. If your lathe has been in service for an extended period of time or you do not know the service history of your lathe, you should consider reconditioning it first. These lathes were originally made to be used continuously in industrial applications, but only with proper care and maintenance can we expect them to last much longer than ourselves.

1945 South Bend 9" Model "A"
This lathe was delivered to the Superior Manufacturing Co. of New York in the late spring of 1945 and still operates flawlessly today. (This Lathe has the War Production Board tag on the lathe bed)

A Brief SBL History

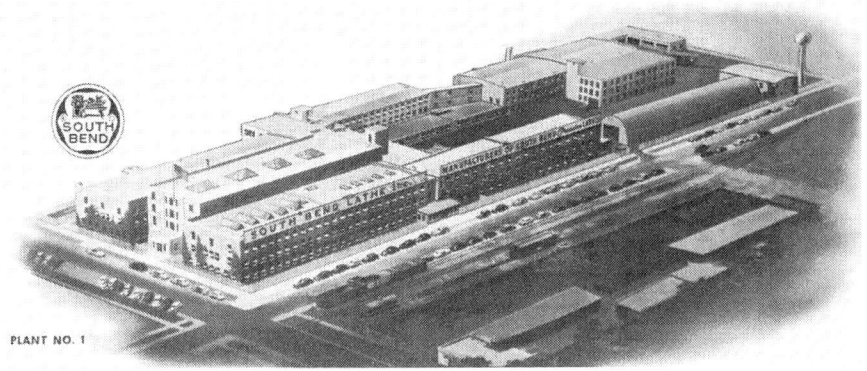

The South Bend Lathe company of Indiana was founded in 1906 by John and Miles O'Brien. The identical twin brothers were born in Ireland and immigrated to the United States at very young age. They grew up and attended school in Indiana and afterwards they spent their early years at the Stanley Tool Works in Connecticut. Miles worked for Thomas Edison briefly, and at Edison's suggestion the two brothers studied engineering at Purdue University. From these experiences, the brothers came up with a new machinists lathe of their own design and they then founded their own company to build it. In 1908 they moved the company to East Madison Street in South Bend and changed the company name to South Bend Lathe Works. For the next 30 years they built the company into one of the most significant manufacturers of industrial lathes in the United States.

During World War II, the company was an important supplier to U.S. defense industries, employing almost 900 workers during that peak time. The newly designed series of 9" workshop lathes and heavy industrial lathes introduced in 1939 were used by the US and its allies to produce essential materials that were supporting the war effort. Because production was critically important to the military, SBL was under the purview of the War Production Board for the duration of the war and all of the company's lathe production was closely controlled and allocated based on WPB needs. All lathes at the time were shipped with a metal tag that read: "Conforms to the Orders of the War Production Board". The company was awarded the U.S. Navy's "E" pennant (Excellence in Production) for their role in the war-time production, putting the company in the top 5% of all U.S. industries. That's how important lathes had become in the 40's.

After the war, the company ramped down production to match the existing market needs, and in 1959 American Steel (soon to become Amsted Industries), bought South Bend Lathe. In 1965, Amsted moved all production to the former Studebaker automobile plant located at 400 W. Sample St in South Bend, where the company remained for the duration of its existence.

In 1975 Amsted decided to close the plant due to a general lack of sales in the machine tool industry which was brought on by poor economic conditions and high interest rates. To try and prevent closure, SBL employees made a gallant effort to keep the company afloat by using a loan from the city of South Bend to form an Employee Stock Ownership Plan and they purchased the company. The ESOP transaction made SBL the first 100% employee-owned corporation in the United States. In 1980 the ESOP vision collapsed when employees represented by United Steelworkers went on strike against their own company over wages and pensions. The company struggled to continue operations until 1992 when South Bend Lathe filed for Chapter 11 bankruptcy and the ESOP was terminated. At that time, the company only had 76 employees remaining.

The business assets changed hands several times after that but SBL never really recovered so segments of the business were sold off over the next 10 years. The company formally closed in May of 2002 and the old Studebaker factory which housed SBL was torn down in May of 2008; a sad ending to a once formidable player in the US machine tool industry. Today, the South Bend name has been rebranded and can be found on many high-quality machine tool imports produced for Grizzly Industrial located in Washington state.

Gone but not forgotten. The South Bend Lathe Factory (Formerly Studebaker) at 400 West Sample St. in 2008, just before demolition.

Lathe Parts Identification

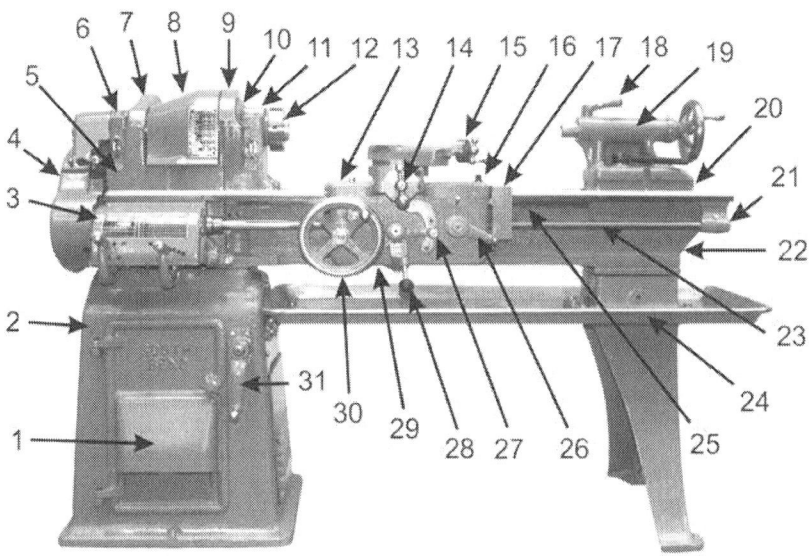

1	Drive Access Door	11	Large Bearing Cap	21	Lead Screw Bracket
2	Cabinet Base	12	Spindle	22	Bed
3	Gearbox	13	Saddle	23	Lead Screw
4	Primary Gear Guard	14	Cross Slide	24	Chip Plan
5	Headstock	15	Compound Slide	25	Rack
6	Small Bearing Cap	16	Saddle Lock	26	Half Nut Cam Lever
7	Quill Guard	17	Threading Dial	27	Shifter Lever
8	Spindle Cone Cover	18	Tailstock Quill Lock	28	ClutchLever (Star Wheel)
9	Bull Gear Guard	19	Tailstock	29	Apron
10	Bull Gear Plunger Guard	20	Tailstock Set-Over Base	30	Apron Handwheel
				31	Belt Tension Crank

Horizontal Drive

1. Motor
2. Horizontal Drive Unit
3. V Belt
4. Counter Shaft
5. Cone Pulley
6. Flat Belt Tension Adjust
7. Back Gear

Observations on General Maintenance

As previously stated, the most significant cause of machine tool wear or failure is the lack of **lubrication** and **cleaning**. Look on ebay at any given time and you will see hundreds of parts for sale that were taken from old South Bends which are being "parted out" (disassembled and sold for parts). While this cringeworthy practice may be seen as a great source for replacement parts which are no longer available, it also means that a vintage working lathe had to be sacrificed to become the organ donor. Why do we see so many old lathes parted out? On one hand the value of the individual parts may be actually greater than the whole lathe but more often than not it is for a completely different reason. Specifically, the one part that you rarely see for sale is the lathe bed... which is because most lathes sent to the chop shop have bed V-ways that are completely worn out and are "sway-backed" which means the center section of the lathe bed has become so worn that the V-ways are lower in the area just in front of the chuck where most of the work is performed. Aside from the spindle, the bed V-ways are the most critical element of the machine and once they are severely damaged, it is difficult to save the lathe. Before the introduction of flame hardened ways (indicated by a "Flame Hardened" tag on the bed) South Bends were primarily "soft iron beds" which meant they were ground, scraped by hand for accuracy and then had geometrical "flaking" applied to the bearing surfaces of the bed to provide recesses for oil retention. When viewing an older machine, if you can still see the original flaking on the bed and it is somewhat uniform, then it has been very well cared for. Excessive wear on the bed as evidenced by deep groves on the

"Flaking" on ways

Heavily scored ways

V-ways means that the lathe was not often cleaned, not adequately lubricated and consequently not well maintained. Turning highly precise work on a lathe in this condition is difficult but it can still be used for general turning where .0005" accuracy is unnecessary.

To help prevent premature bed wear, when turning iron or other "gritty" materials it is absolutely essential to either keep the lathe bed covered with a cloth, or clean and lubricate the ways frequently. Since the bed is the part which is most exposed to the "elements" during operation, just using lots of oil on the ways is not sufficient. Mixing large amounts of oil with iron particles makes a great lapping compound so there is another line of defense: the felt *Way Wipers*. These four tiny components are absolutely the cheapest and easiest to replace part on the lathe, yet they are the single most overlooked maintenance item by far *and* the most detrimental if ignored.

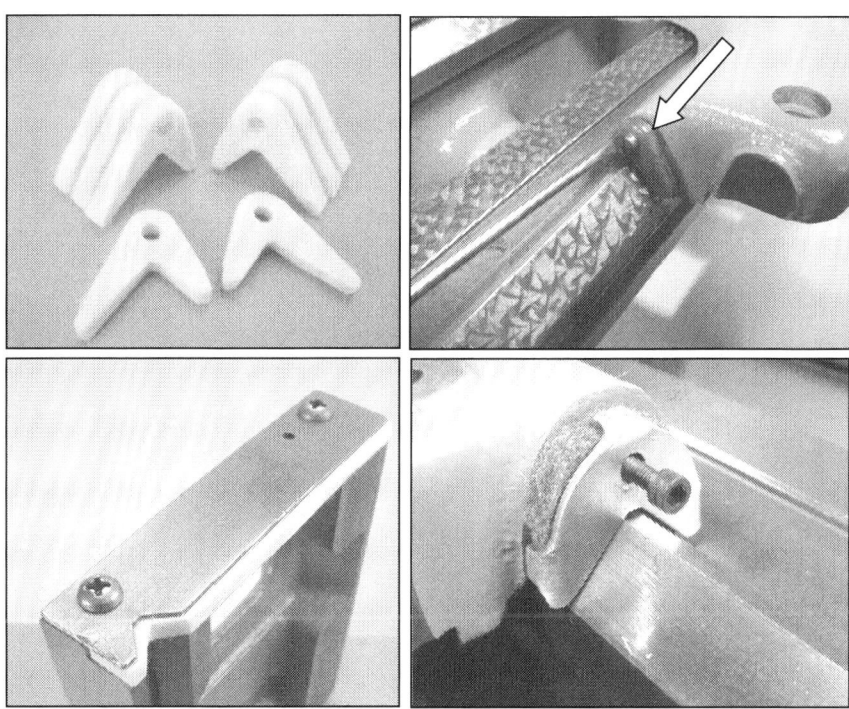

Top Left: New felt way wipers used on the 9" and model 10k lathes.
Top Right: Brass "keeper" and screw that secures the way wiper.
Bottom Right: Brass Keeper on a 13" Lathe. Note the shape of the wiper and that it must compressed against the bed to form a tight seal.
Bottom Left: Felt Tailstock Wiper (Used on larger industrial lathes)

The way wipers are made from hard, die-cut felt which is precisely sized to fit the profile of the lathe bed V-ways or flats. The wipers serve two purposes. First, wipers act as a primary filter to catch and prevent any dirt or turning debris from entering the gap between the lathe saddle and the bed where it can cause damage. Second, the wipers act as a wick to absorb and retain the heavy way oil so that the saddle and bed bearing surfaces have a constant supply of oil during use. Wipers are held in place by steel or brass "keepers". Maintenance is literally removing the one screw on each keeper, replacing the felt wipers and then reinstalling the screws. The operation is 10 minutes maximum. Since every size of South Bend Lathe had different sized ways, every lathe had its own specially designed wiper set that compressed tightly against the v-way. If you decide to make your own instead of buying them, make sure to cut them slightly oversize so that they will compress against the V-way surface once installed. If they are not a snug fit, then they will not prevent contaminants from entering the saddle bearing surfaces. If you don't replace the wipers with new ones periodically, at least remove and clean them in a suitable solvent before re-oiling them.

It is truly remarkable that so many South Bends are still running today so if we intend to pass these tools to our grandchildren, we must recognize that the lathe bed and saddle are the Achilles heel on any South Bend. **Watch Those Wipers and Keep Them Clean!**

The Bare Minimum:

Since most lathes found in home shops are only used periodically and for very short durations, it is difficult to develop a maintenance routine because it is not practiced every day. Rather than belabor the details, if you remember nothing else from this manual, at the very least remember do this prior to each and every use:

1. **Oil the spindle bearing**
2. **Oil the counter-shaft drive bearings**
3. **Wipe down and oil the V-ways & wipers.**

Just doing these three things will greatly extend the life of the tool and though it may not guarantee another 100 years of constant operation, the lathe will at least be given a fighting chance to survive your stewardship.

Safe Practices

As with any machine operation, the maintenance should always be undertaken with the correct personal safety equipment. Please note that safe practices today are not what they were in the 1940's.

Safety Glasses: If you'll notice from old publications and photos, safety glasses were rarely used 75 years ago. You may also notice that on most of the older wooden machinists' tool chests, there was a mirror mounted on the inside cover and more often than not, one would also find a small magnet stuck to the metal frame nearby. That mirror was there for a reason. It assisted the machinist with removing metal chips if they happened to get one stuck in their eye. Do not laugh, most old timers always kept a small magnet nearby for that reason and it was very effective... at least for ferrous metals. Brass was a different story. Today we tend to behave proactively through the use of proper safety glasses rather than being reactive and dealing with an injury after it happens. At the very minimum, current ANSI Z87 approved safety glasses or goggles should be worn at all times when operating or performing maintenance on the lathe. Small metal chips are the equivalent of tiny razors, so you really want to avoid a trip to the emergency room because a small chip was ejected straight into your eye. A magnet is "Plan B" only.

Clothing: Avoid long sleeves or loose clothing that can become ensnared in the chuck, workpiece or in the open lathe gearing. Most older lathes did not always have belt guards or other covers to prevent contact with open gearing or pulleys, so loose clothing can be easily grabbed by the machine and it is difficult to avoid injury if that happens. No rings, or jewelry! If a ring is accidentally caught in the moving machinery, the finger will unfortunately surrender before the ring will. Gloves should be worn when removing metal chips and spiral steel ribbons. Steel ribbons are razor-sharp and should always be handled with care.

Wear Safety Glasses !!

Cleaning the Lathe

The Importance of Regular Cleaning

The short amount of time required to properly clean the lathe after each use contributes significantly to extending the life of your vintage iron. Turning accuracy is retained indefinitely if the basics of proper lubrication and good housekeeping practices are always observed. If chips and dirt are allowed to accumulate on the V-ways, dovetails, or other critical bearing surfaces, it will cause accelerated wear and the service life of the lathe will be prematurely cut short.

Unless vacuumed or brushed away frequently, grit and other metal particles produced by the cutting tool will combine with the lubricants and form a black sludge over time. Because this sludge is extremely abrasive, it increases sliding friction making the controls harder to operate, and it will accelerate wear on the bearing surfaces.

If sludge is permitted to collect under the tailstock, saddle or in the spindle taper, the turning accuracy of the lathe will be reduced. Small chips from most tool steels are especially damaging because they are extremely hard and sharp and they may actually cut into the bearing surfaces over time if not removed. Be aware that cast iron, bronze and other sand-cast metals are harmful to bearings because of the inherent scale and residual sand that is left behind from the metal casting process. These materials tend to remain on the surface of the metal. Always cover the ways and other exposed bearing surfaces when machining these metals, especially during the initial cuts.

The Importance of Chip Removal

Regular removal of the chips produced during the turning operation is essential to maintaining the lathe. If the metal chips are allowed to accumulate, they become a hazard for both the machine and the operator. Steel ribbons from the turning process are razor sharp and must be removed carefully. If these ribbons are not removed, they can be grabbed by the revolving chuck and act as a flail to beat the operator to death. Not really, but you can get hurt. A long hook should be used to remove the ribbons from around the chuck and tool post if they become entangled. Never use bare hands when cleaning out metal shavings and never try to remove them when the lathe is still running. Severe lacerations or other injuries may result.

Use a Vacuum and Brush

A small shop vacuum with a crevice tool is a great asset to have close by for cleaning the lathe. The object is to actually REMOVE the chips and debris from the work area and not just move them around. A small paint brush when used in conjunction the shop vac works well for dislodging debris that tends to stick to the oily lathe surfaces. Keep the vacuum nozzle close the area being brushed in order to capture as much debris as possible.

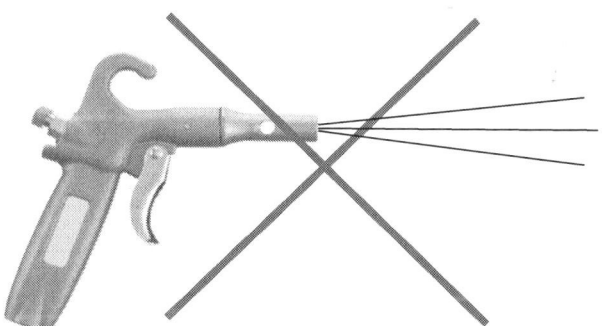

NEVER Use Compressed Air to Clean the Lathe

Compressed air should never be used for cleaning the lathe because it will blow dirt and chips deep into oil passages and bearing surfaces where they cannot be easily removed without disassembling the lathe. Compressed air is also a hazard as it can dislodge chips and dirt and propel them toward the operator causing possible injury.

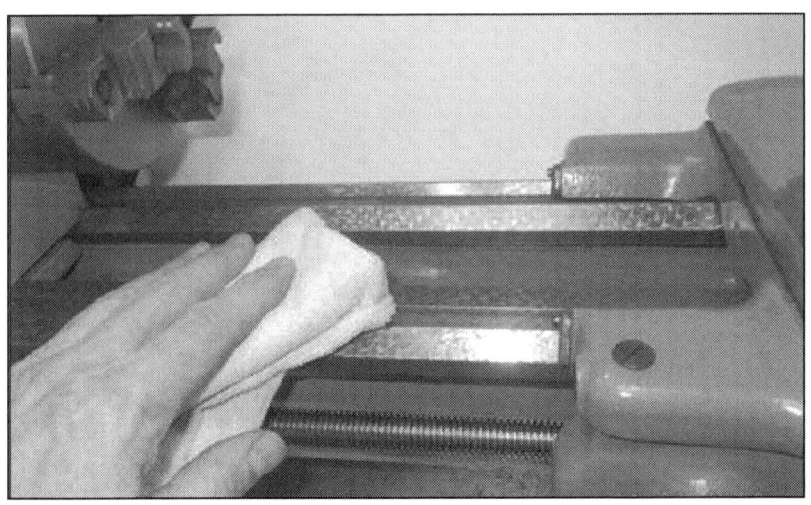

Wipe Down the Lathe

A clean cloth can be used, after vacuuming and brushing, to remove any remaining residue. A small amount of general-purpose oil on the cloth will prevent surface rust from forming. Always stop the lathe before using the cloth to avoid the possibility of the cloth becoming snagged in the moving parts. In regular use the lathe should be thoroughly cleaned with a mild solvent. WD-40 works very well for general cleaning since it is mostly solvent and it will not damage the painted surfaces. WD-40 should not be used as a protective coating or lubricant so only use light oil for that purpose. Do not use caustic cleaners or chemicals with chlorine in them as it can cause the iron to rust. Very fine Scotch-brite pads or steel wool can be used for removing surface rust but since these pads contain fine abrasives, the lathe should be cleaned very carefully and re-oiled after using.

Inspect the Lathe Before Each Use

The lathe should be inspected periodically in order to detect any problems so that they can be fixed before they become more serious. As mentioned previously, the bed V-ways can be damaged by metal contaminants imbedded in the saddle or tailstock base. If you see any new scoring on the V-ways (or flats) that was not present before or if you see black sticky streaks on the V-ways from oily contaminants, the lathe saddle and tailstock base should be removed, all surfaces cleaned and new oiled wipers should be installed. Do not wait!

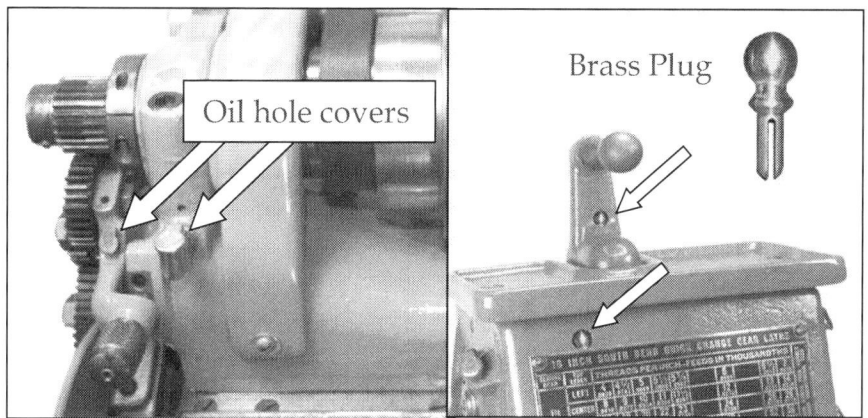

All oil fill ports should have covers which may consist of brass plugs or the "Gits" type oil hole covers (with spring-loaded caps) to prevent contaminants from entering the lathe internals. If an oil hole cover is broken or missing, it should be replaced immediately.

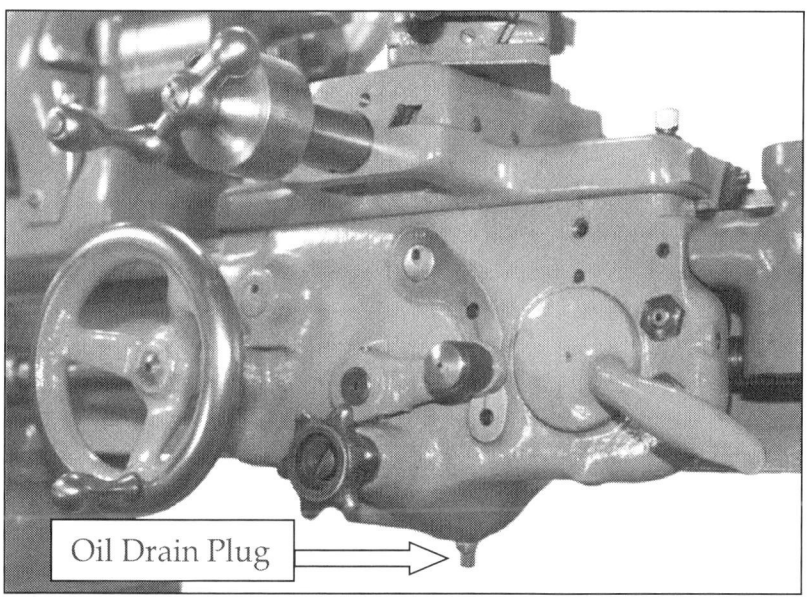

The apron oil reservoir acts very much like the oil pan on a car and the oil needs to be changed periodically. The reservoir should be drained and cleaned by flushing it with kerosene every 1-2 years depending on the frequency of use. The apron uses the same oil as the spindle. Use Teflon tape on the plug threads to prevent leaks.

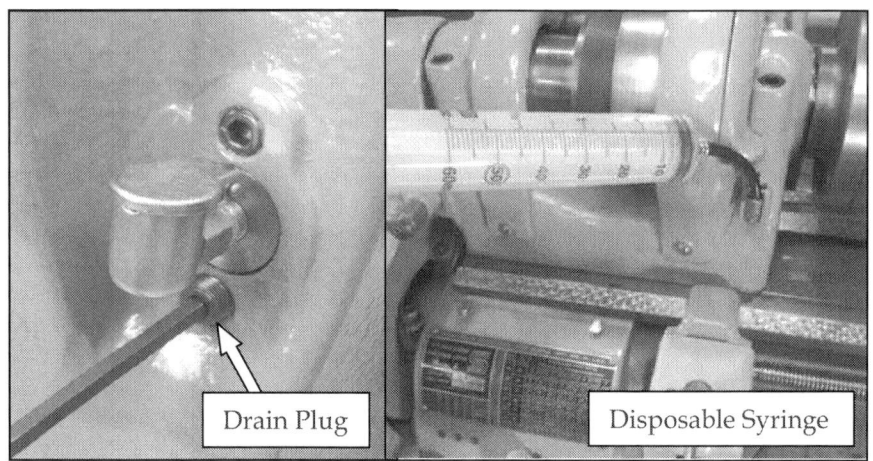

Drain Plug   Disposable Syringe

In regular use, the headstock oil reservoirs should also be drained and flushed 2-3 times with clean oil every year. If there is a drain plug beneath the oil cups as shown above, the reservoir can be drained directly. If not, a large disposable syringe with a rubber tube works very well for siphoning the oil out through the oil fill cups. Do not put solvents in the headstock reservoirs as it will be very difficult to remove that solvent from the capillary oilers inside the headstock. Top off the fill cups with fresh spindle oil after flushing.

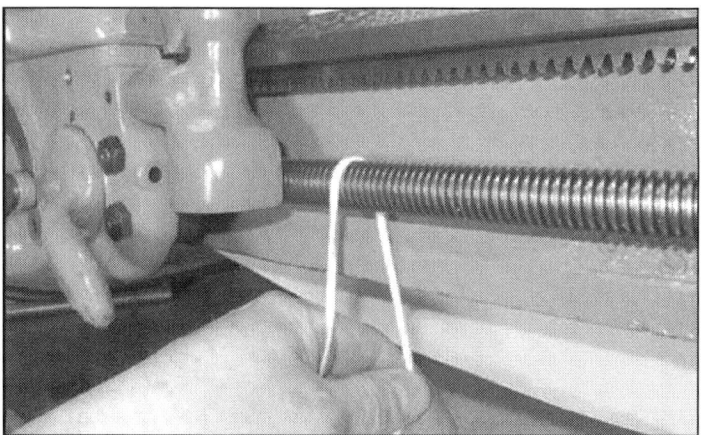

Metal chips and dirt should not be allowed to build up on the threads of the lead screw, the headstock gear-train, or quick-change gearbox. An easy way to clean the threads of the lead screw is to hold a pipe cleaner or stiff cotton cord soaked in solvent in the thread groove and pull the ends back and forth as the lead screw revolves slowly.

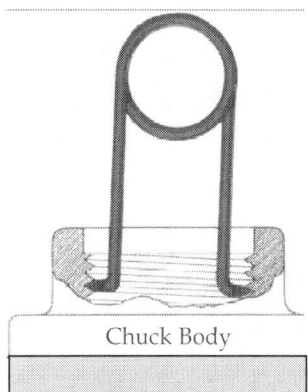

Chuck Body

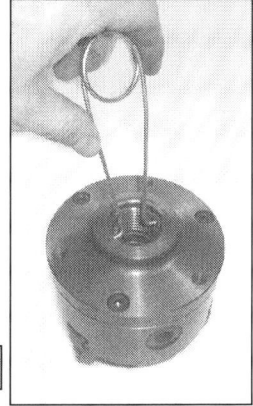

Left: Clean the chuck and spindle thread with a cleaning tool before mounting the chuck.
Below: If the chuck is seized, lock the spindle using a strap wrench, and chuck a hexagonal piece of stock in the jaws. Use a large wrench on the hexagonal stock to loosen the chuck.

Clean the Spindle Nose and Chuck Threads

The threads and mounting collar on the lathe spindle should be cleaned regularly and lightly oiled before mounting a chuck or a face plate on the spindle nose. The threads in the back of the face plate or chuck should also be cleaned carefully. A heavy steel wire bent to the shape shown above works very well. The tips of the wire should be ground to match the V shape of the thread groove. Tiny chips or particles on the spindle or chuck threads will prevent the chuck from seating properly and the chuck will not run true. If there are chips in the thread, they can also cause the chuck to seize on the spindle. If the chuck is seized, place a large strap wrench on the cone pulley as shown. Mount a piece of hexagonal stock in the 3-jaw chuck and unscrew it with a large wrench. Chucks are always right-hand thread so turn towards the operator. **DO NOT** use the back-gear as a spindle lock since the stress can result in broken teeth on the gears.

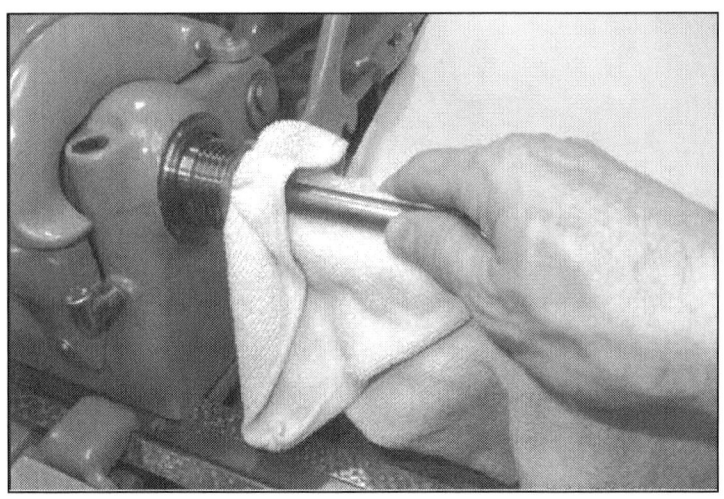

Clean the Spindle Tapers

Tapers are essentially conical wedges and they cannot fit together properly unless they are absolutely clean and free from dirt or burrs. Any small defect will throw the taper out of true and it will not hold the tool securely. A cloth wrapped around a wooden dowel rod is perfect for cleaning the taper holes in the headstock and tailstock spindles. A cylindrical bottle brush also makes a great cleaning tool. After cleaning, do not lubricate the tapers with oil because they will not hold properly. **Never, insert your finger into the taper of the spindle while the lathe is running!** It is tempting to put a rag on your finger and stick it in the spindle hole while it is turning but you do not want to think about the consequences if the cloth snags or wedges in the spindle with your finger inside. Dead centers and drill chucks shanks should be wiped with a clean cloth before installing them in the spindle taper. A slight rap with a wooden or hard rubber mallet is sufficient to seat a taper so if it does not seat properly, inspect all taper surfaces. If the dead center, collet sleeve or a drill chuck does not run true then the taper may be the cause.

Clean the Saddle and Tool Holder

The compound rest, cross slide and tool holders should always be kept clean since most chips are generated in this area. Small chips underneath the tool holder may prevent the cutting tool from having the solid support necessary for taking a smooth cut and the tool may chatter. An unsupported cutting tool may also break under stress.

 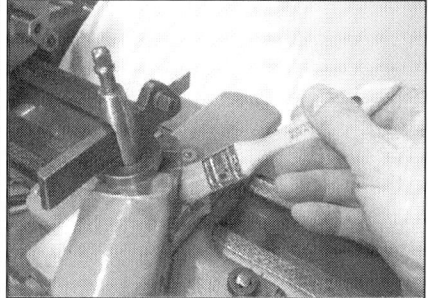

The dovetails of both the compound rest and cross slide assembly should be kept free from chips and dirt. If the dovetail surface become dirty, it will cause the dovetails to bind, making them difficult to move smoothly. Chips or dirt between the compound base and the swivel may also cause the lathe to chatter.

Flat Belt

Drive V Belt

Clean the Belts

Oil and dirt may cause the belts (especially flat belts) to slip which damages the belt and causes a loss of power to the spindle. The Drive V-belts and Flat Belt on the cone pulley should be kept clean and free from oil, dirt, and chips. Any mild degreasing cleaner such as Formula 409 will work fine and not damage the belts. Scrub and dry thoroughly before use. If you are still using a flat leather belt, a preservative like neatsfoot oil will keep the leather pliable but it must dry thoroughly. Belt dressings should not be used since they act as an adhesive film for dirt and chips. When the belt tension is adjusted correctly, a clean flat belt will transmit all necessary power required for machining any work within the capacity of the lathe.

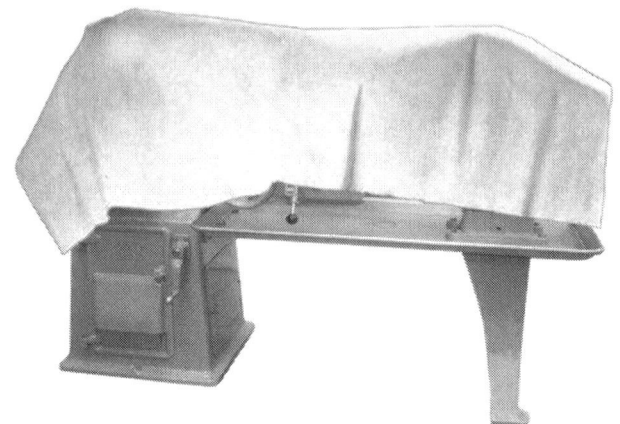

Protecting the Lathe in the Shop

Abrasive dust will cause serious damage if it gets into the lathe bearings but it is difficult to prevent in most machine shops. Though lathe tool post grinders are shown in many period publications, using one on a vintage lathe is not a good idea. If it is necessary to install a tool post grinder on the lathe, or a surface or bench grinder near the lathe, a vacuum dust collection system is essential and the ways and carriage should be fully covered with a shop cloth when the grinder is in use. A Velcro strap with a strip of cloth can be wrapped around the spindle nose to prevent dust from entering the spindle bearing. The entire lathe should be thoroughly cleaned and wiped down after the grinding operation is completed.

Lathes in Unconditioned Shops

When the lathe is not in use it should be covered with a cloth tarp or blanket to protect it. In shops without heating and cooling, it will be necessary to take precautions to prevent surface rust from forming on bare metal parts. Typically, the worst condition is when the lathe is cooler than its surroundings and it then comes in contact with warm, moist air. Moisture will condense on the exposed bare metal surfaces and cause surface rust. If left untreated, pitting and damage may occur over time. A very simple method for preventing this is to put a small heat source under the lathe cover to always keep the lathe a couple of degrees warmer that its surroundings. A "GoldenRod" dehumidifier is a small electrically heated bar that works very well. Place the bar underneath the lathe cover when the lathe is not in use.

Lubricating the Lathe

The Importance of Proper Lubrication

Maintenance of the oils and the oil delivery systems within the lathe is critical to preserving a vintage machine. Most South Bend Lathes have internal oil reservoirs, felt wicks, and oil retainers to guard against oil starvation due to temporary neglect. Lathes produced before the 1930's rarely had these wicks and felts so they used what is called a "complete loss" oiling system. The oil cups were filled each day and the oil gradually ran out over time. Very messy but effective in keeping the bearings flushed with clean oil.

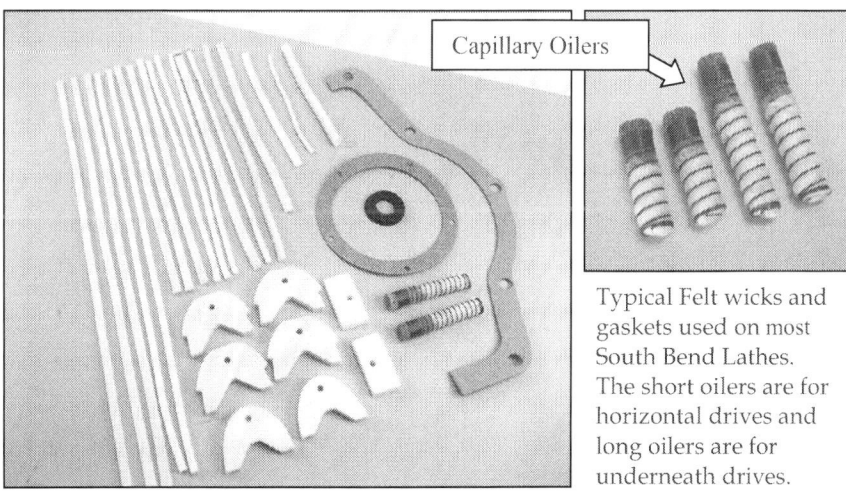

Capillary Oilers

Typical Felt wicks and gaskets used on most South Bend Lathes. The short oilers are for horizontal drives and long oilers are for underneath drives.

The purpose of the lubricants is to minimize friction between moving parts and to prevent metal-to-metal bearing surfaces from wearing due to abrasion. The lubricant forms a protective film which acts as a cushion between the bearing surfaces. In a perfect world there would be no metal to metal contact but as the machine is put under load, this contact cannot be avoided so the more uniform the oil film, the less friction there is. If the bearings are run dry or the oil film breaks down, there will be nothing to separate the bearing surfaces and they may become scored or badly damaged in a very short period of time. It is important that all bearings and bearing surfaces receive a constant supply of clean oil.

Use the Correct Type of Oil

The type of oil used for each application in the lathe is often overlooked. Machine oils are specifically engineered to perform based on their respective viscosities, which is simply a measure of how the oil resists flow at a set temperature. Spindles use much thinner viscosity oils since they must perform at higher speeds and if a thicker oil were to be used, the spindle would start to overheat due to the added friction from the thicker oil's resistance to flow. In a spindle, the "bearing" is actually a film of oil that is dynamically distributed during the rotation. The spindle at rest actually settles to the bottom of the bearing since the oil alone cannot support the weight. As the spindle begins to rotate, the oil film is distributed over the bearing surface and the spindle starts to ride atop the oil film and it then self-centers in the bearing shell. The amount of clearance between the spindle and the bearing is very small but this gap is very important for the spindle oil to perform properly. If the gap is too small the bearing will be starved for oil. If the gap is too large, excessive oil will be used and the spindle will move within the bearing which will affect accuracy. More on that later...

In most South Bend Lathe publications of the period, you may see oils referenced as Type A, Type B or Type C. "Type" has no meaning other than to easily differentiate the oils and the letters ABC simply correspond to a specific oil grade. Suggested modern oil equivalents may be found on the following page. Never use automotive engine oils. Engine oils are designed to work at much higher temperatures and they have detergents and other additives which may cause damage to the lathe bearings and other surfaces.

Machine Oil Specifications for South Bend Lathes

Units are in Saybolt Universal Seconds Viscosity at 100°F

Type A (Spindle): 100 seconds (Mobil Velocite 10 ISO 22)
Type B (Gearbox / Drive): 150-240 seconds (Mobil DTE, ISO 32)
Type C (General Purpose): 250-500 seconds (Mobil DTE, ISO 68)
Way Oil: 300-500 seconds (Mobil Vactra Medium Way)

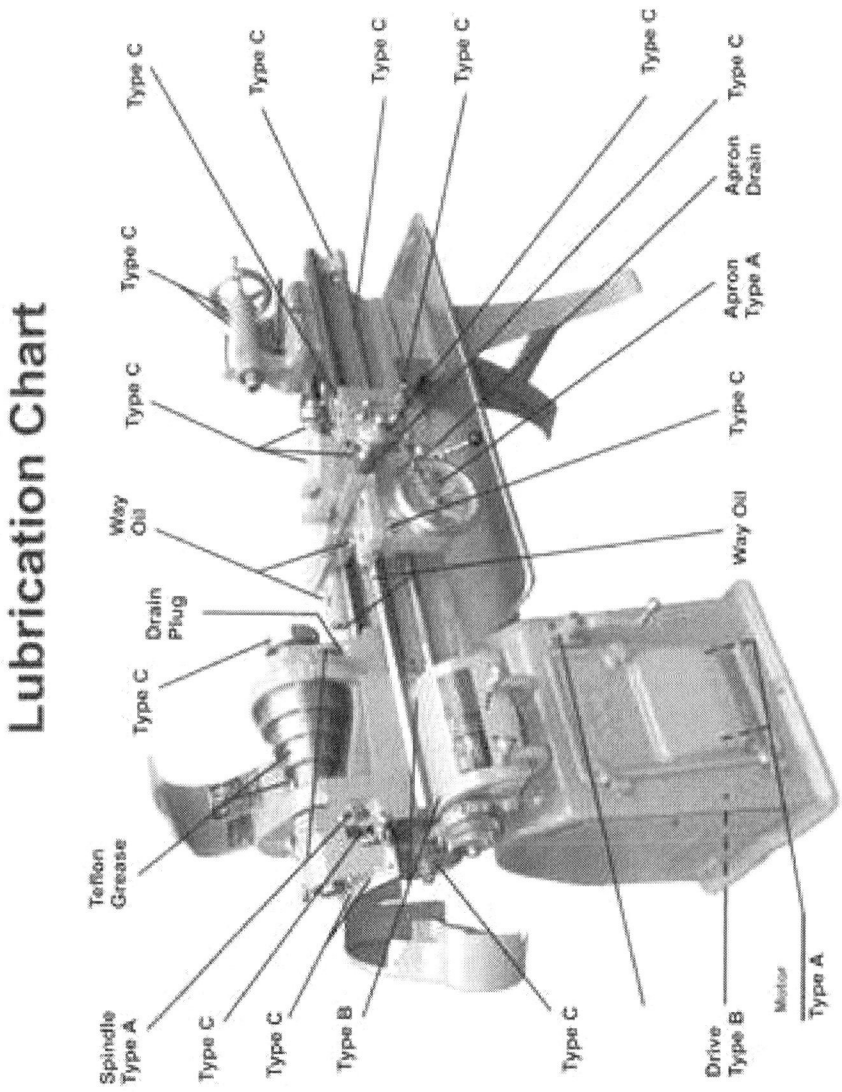

Oil Wicks and Oil Retention Felt

As mentioned previously, later model South Bends typically use dense wool felt for wicks, wipers and capillary oilers in order to provide lubrication and oil retention to critical machine components. Felt is engineered very much like the oils and it is important to use the correct felt sizes in the correct grade based on the lubrication requirements. Felt wicks are primarily used to transmit oil from the oil fill port to the bearings but they perform other functions as well. The felt acts as a filter by trapping outside contaminants in the wool fibers yet they allow the oil to pass by freely as long as they do not become overly dirty. The felt in contact with bearing surfaces also absorbs and retains oil so that the surface tension of the oil is used to keep it in the bearing instead of allowing it to run out. South Bend added oil retention felt to many of its lathe designs in the late 1930's to make them more reliable, which was a very important feature as more and more unskilled machinist entered the workforce during WWII. When oil recirculation reservoirs and oil retention felts were used, it was much more difficult to damage a lathe because the operator forgot to fill one of the oil cups at the start of the shift. Maintenance had to be neglected for days before it actually became a problem. These features account for the "bullet-proof" nature of the lathes and were a clever bit of engineering that can be credited for saving many of the South Bend Lathes that are still around today.

The density and performance of the felt wicks is just as important as the lubricants that they carry. Felt is graded based on the type of wool used, plus the density and compression properties. Felt can be purchased in many different grades but SAE F1 (hard white felt) and SAE F3 (medium hard gray felt) are the two most commonly found felts in South Bend Lathes. The F1 hard felt is very durable and wicks the oil very slowly, but it also retains that oil for a much longer period of time and allows it to continuously provide some small amount of oil to the bearing. The less dense F3 felt wicks the oil more quickly but it also gives up the oil quickly so it needs to be replenished more often. For these reasons, most of the oil retention felts and wicks are made from F1 hard felt and the capillary oil wicks are softer F3 felt. Long strand loose wool "packing" can also be found in the base of the capillary oilers and in some of the older drives where the capillary action is very fast and very large amounts of oil can be supplied to the drive bearings.

 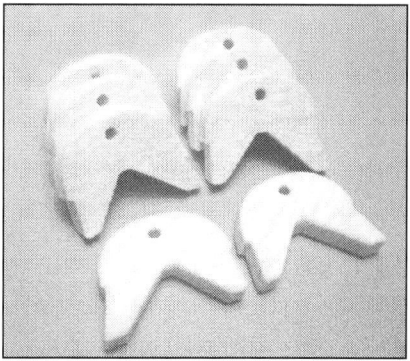

The components of the capillary oilers used for spindle lubrication are shown above left. Essentially the white stranded packing soaks up the oil in the bottom of the reservoir and feeds it to the cylindrical gray felt plug on top which is held in contact with the spindle by the force of the spring. Since this lubrication method relies on an oil reservoir inside the headstock, the capillary oilers are engineered to supply spindle oil at a very high rate and the oil is then returned to the reservoir and recirculated. Capillary oilers were added to all South Bend Lathes during the late 1930s so lathes produced prior to this time only had the gravity feed oil fill cups on top of the bearing caps. The fill cups on top of the bearing caps are a quick indicator of the lathe vintage. Later model lathes with capillary oilers will have the elbow shaped fill cups located on the front side of the headstock.

Shown above right is the typical hard white F1 felt; used for wipers and wicks where durability and long oil retention is required.

As with the Lubricants, South Bend used different "Types" of felts which indicated the size only. The "Types" are all F1 Hard Felt and represent lengths of rectangular felt strip or round felt cord.

Felt Wicks and Wipers:

Type 1......................... 1/16" x 1/8" rectangular cross section
Type 2......................... 1/16" x 3/16" rectangular cross section
Type 3......................... 3/32" x 3/16" rectangular cross section
Type 7......................... 3/16" Round cross section
Type 13.......................1/8" x 1/4" rectangular cross section
Type 14.......................1/8" Round cross section
Tailstock Wipers.............3/16" Die Cut Felt F1 Felt
Way Wipers...................1/4", 3/16" or 5/32" Die Cut F1 Felt

The Oiling Routine in 5 Steps

The lathe should always be stopped before oiling. All oiling ports should be filled or checked at least once a day during normal operation or more often when running at higher spindle speeds and feed rates. At higher speeds, lubricants tend to fly off into space, therefore more frequent lubrication may be required under these conditions. The best practice is to fill each oiling port in the same order every time so that the operation becomes a habit and it will be less likely that a lubrication point will be missed. Always clean around the oiling ports with a shop cloth prior to opening the cap or plug so that contaminants do not fall into the oil passages. To assist with the maintenance routine and to make it easy to identify the correct oil grade, the caps on the oil hole covers can be painted a bright color to make them easy to identify. Different colors of paint may be used to indicate the type of oil to use at that location. If you do not want to paint your vintage Gits Oil Hole Covers, you can use easy-to-remove colored vinyl "dots" that can be found at most office supply stores. Just clean the cap well before applying the dots.

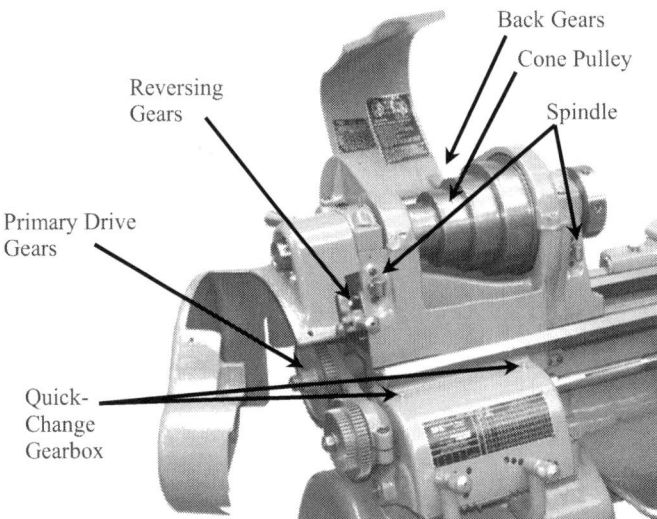

Step 1: The Headstock

The locations of the oil holes for lubricating the lathe headstock are shown above. There is an oil reservoir in the headstock beneath each of the two spindle bearings. These reservoirs should be filled daily with **Type A** oil. The oil level should be 1/8" from the top rim.

Spindle Lubrication

Later model South Bend Lathes have what is referred to in their marketing brochures as "superfinished" spindles. The process for "superfinishing" consisted of carburizing the spindle, hardening it to a Rockwell C scale of 58, and then fine-grinding it to a surface finish of 5 µ-inches (.000005") smoothness. The bearings in the headstock were similarly finished and the two parts were fitted with "extreme precision". As mentioned earlier, the gap for the spindle oil film is very small because of these tight tolerances, so a light spindle oil such as Mobil Velocite 10 (**Type A**) is highly recommended. A good way to tell if a lathe is equipped with a "superfinished" spindle is to check for the presence of a brass lubrication plate on the headstock or primary gear cover specifying the lubricants. Note that older lathe models from the 1920's and early 1930's with oil cups on top of headstock bearing caps do not have superfinished spindles so the bearing clearances are slightly larger. Always use a medium weight machine oil such as the "**Type B**" for lubricating the spindle bearings on all lathes with oil cups on top of the bearing caps.

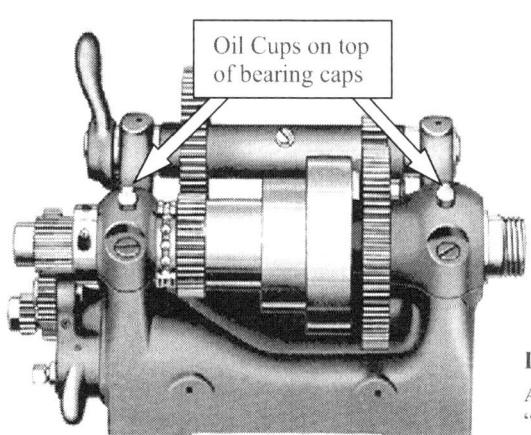
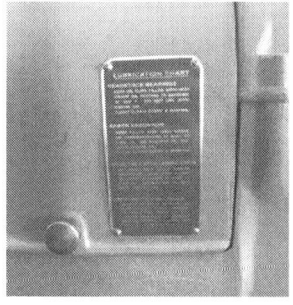

Left: Oil Cups on bearing caps
Above: Lubrication Plate for a "Superfinished" Spindle

On any lathe, if the spindle bearings heat above 120° Fahrenheit (or the bearing cap becomes uncomfortably hot to the touch), it is an indication that either the oil is too heavy, the bearing clearances are too tight, or the oil has become dirty. If heating occurs, the lathe should be stopped immediately, the spindle bearings flushed, and the reservoirs filled with clean spindle oil. If heating persists, see the section later in this book on how to set the spindle bearing clearance.

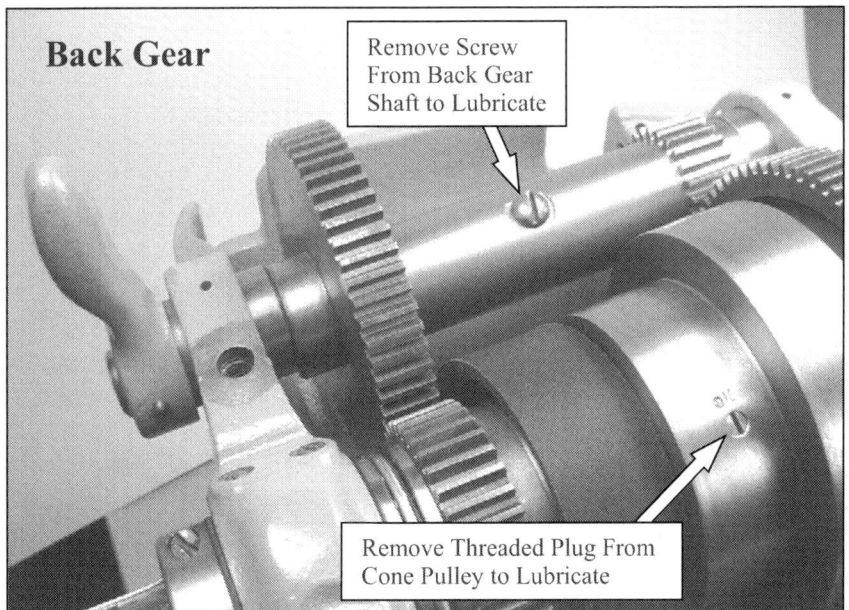

Back Gear

The back gear and the cone pulley bearings should be lubricated periodically. There is often confusion on this topic since early models had the word "OIL" stamped near the fill plug and later models had the word "GREASE" stamped in the same location. The back gear bearing clearances are such that either heavy machine oil "**Type C**" or light Teflon grease may be used for either application though light grease is recommended because it will stay in the bearing much longer and does not require the constant maintenance. If the back gear feature is not often used, then regular lubrication is not necessary. It is best practice to lubricate the cone pulley and back gear quill just before engaging the back gear since it minimizes excess heavy oil or grease collecting near the spindle. Oil and grease from filling the cone pulley exits just beside the spindle bearings. If the excess grease or heavy oil enters the spindle bearings, it could contaminate the lighter spindle oil and cause overheating & damage.

Grease: SBL originally specified a light Teflon grease made by Roy Dean Products which is no longer available. In the late 1990's SBL started shipping "Super Lube" synthetic grease as a substitute and though it is thicker and runs slightly warmer than the Roy Dean grease, it works very well for the back gear quill and cone pulleys.

Reversing Gears

The reversing gears or "twin gears" are part of the primary gear train and are located on the left side of the headstock casting. In regular operation, these gears should be lubricated daily with the "**Type C**" oil. The reversing gears simply provide a method for transmitting power from the spindle to the primary gear train and for reversing the rotation direction of the lead screw by simply shifting the position of the twin gears on the spindle.

There are two styles of reversing gears. The style used on earlier lathes simply had two oil passages drilled into the ends of the gear shafts and oil was squirted into those holes to provide lubrication to the gears. Later models were more complex and had oil passages drilled inside the castings and these models used felt cord inside to transfer the oil to the bearing surfaces on the face of the gears as well as the gear shafts and pivot shaft on the gear carrier. The later models can be identified by the oil hole covers located just above the reversing handle. For either type, fill the reservoirs to the top of the hole or cup. It is not necessary to oil the gear teeth or gear faces beyond just a light coating to protect the metal surfaces from rust. Periodically remove the gear carrier from the headstock so that the spring-loaded stops and pivot shaft may be cleaned and re-oiled.

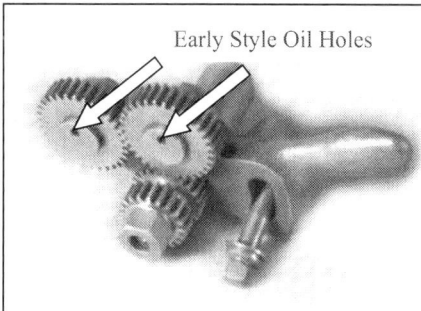

Above Left: Late 9" model reversing gears with plunger stop.

Above Right: 1950's model reversing gears with lever stop.

Left: Early 10" model reversing gears with oiling holes in the shafts. Note the bolt that locks the gear bracket in place instead of the later plunger and lever stops which were much easier to engage.

Step 2: The Change Gear Mechanism

South Bend used several different change gear configurations on their lathes over the years. The oldest style is the manual change gear arrangement which uses a set of loose gears with varying numbers of teeth that require the operator to change each gear in the gear train in order to obtain the desired feed rates or thread pitch. On later models, SBL introduced "quick-change" gear boxes which only required the operator to move a lever "or tumbler" to achieve the desired thread or feed. Of the quick-change variants, there was the early single-tumbler model that had an individual oil holes for each bearing. The later quick-change gearboxes have 2 oil cups on top of the case that distribute oil to the bearings through internal passages.

If the gearbox is a single-tumbler model with an oil hole on the front as shown below, place the plunger in the first hole on the left before oiling. In this position the tumbler is aligned with the oiling tube which lubricates the tumbler bearings. In any other position the tumbler bearing will not receive any oil. If the gearbox is a single tumbler model, but the tumbler oil hole is on the right side of the body, place the plunger in the third hole from the right before oiling. On double tumbler gearboxes, the tumblers can be in any position during oiling. In normal use, fill all oil cups daily with **Type B** oil. Make sure all oil ports are closed before operation. Note: For all models, the idler and compound gear on the gear banjo should be oiled by way of the hole provide in the collar of the gear (see below).

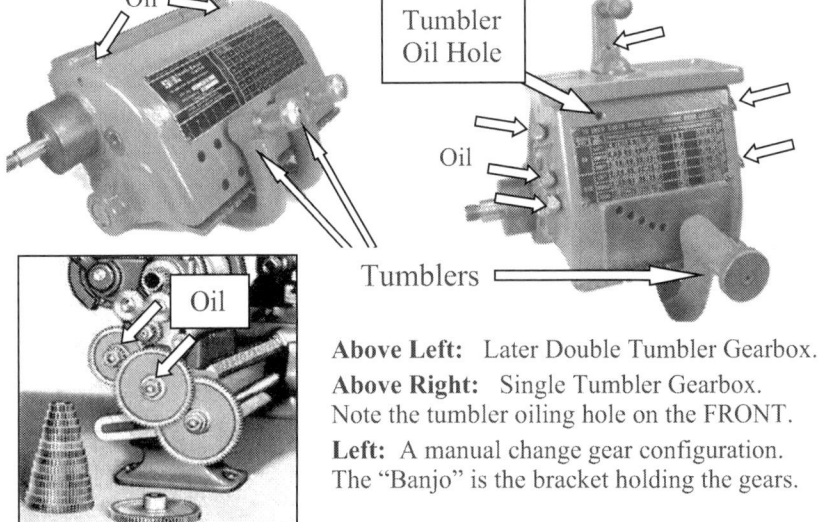

Above Left: Later Double Tumbler Gearbox.
Above Right: Single Tumbler Gearbox.
Note the tumbler oiling hole on the FRONT.
Left: A manual change gear configuration. The "Banjo" is the bracket holding the gears.

Step 3: The Carriage (Saddle & Apron)

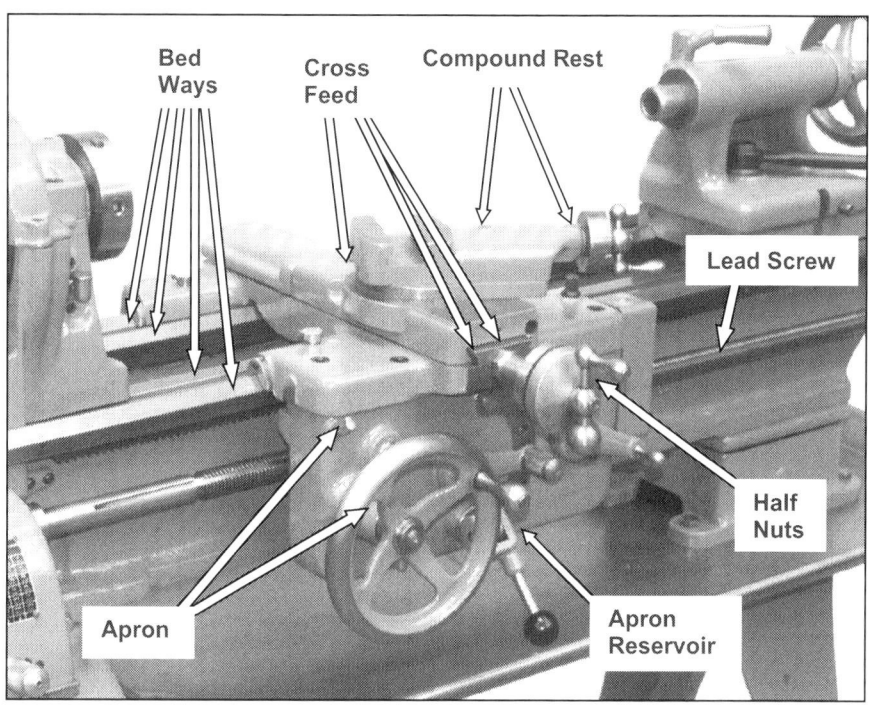

The locations of the oil holes for lubricating the various bearings on the saddle and apron are shown above. Type A Spindle oil should be used for the apron reservoir, Medium Way Oil for the bed V-ways, and Type C for all other oiling points. A large oil reservoir is located in the bottom of the apron and it supplies oil for the apron clutch and internal gears for all of the powered feeds. The oil for the reservoir is filled through the "elbow-shaped" oil cup at the bottom of the apron. The oil level should be checked daily and maintained within 1/8 inch of the top rim of the oil cup. A number of felt wicks carry the oil from the reservoir to critical bearings in the apron. The apron oil reservoir should be drained, flushed with kerosene, and refilled with every 1-2 years depending on the frequency of use.

Spindle oil is specified for the apron because of the disk-type clutch mechanism used for engaging the power feeds. When the star hand wheel (or lever on later models) is engaged, the clutch disks are squeezed together and the friction between them will drive the carriage feeds. Heavier oil will cause the clutch to slip or not release properly so be careful not to use heavier oils in the apron reservoir.

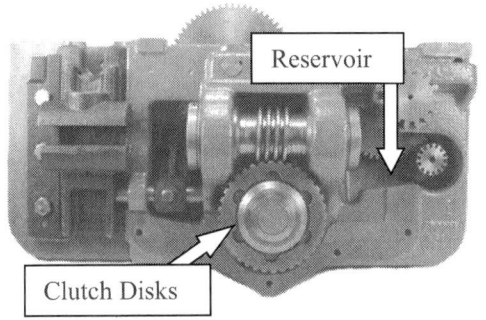

Rear view of the apron with the reservoir cover removed, showing the clutch pack and the internal gears that require lubrication. Long felt strips are used as wicks to transfer oil from the reservoir to all of the various bearings by using capillary action.

If heavy oil is used by accident; it will be necessary to drain the oil reservoir and refill with it a 50/50 mixture of kerosene and Type A oil. Run the lathe power feeds for a short time, drain the mixture and refill with fresh Type A oil.

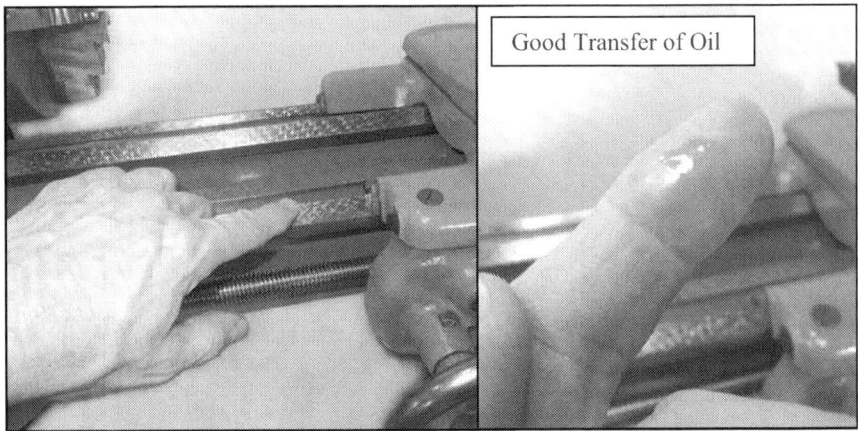

Because of the high usage, all of the carriage gibs, handwheels and the bed V ways should be lubricated with machine oil every time the lathe is used. In order to tell if there is sufficient oil on the bed V ways, lightly touch it with your finger. If oil transfers visibly then there is sufficient oil. If oil is not visible, re-oil the ways and move the carriage back and forth to distribute the oil. The cross-feed and compound rest screw bearings have threaded plugs which must be removed for oiling. A needle tip oiler should be used and inserted fully into these holes. If the oil can has a large tip, air cannot escape and the oil will not enter the hole. The lead screw threads should be oiled frequently when cutting screw threads. The oil hole for the lead screw bearing at the right end of the lathe bed should be oiled daily.

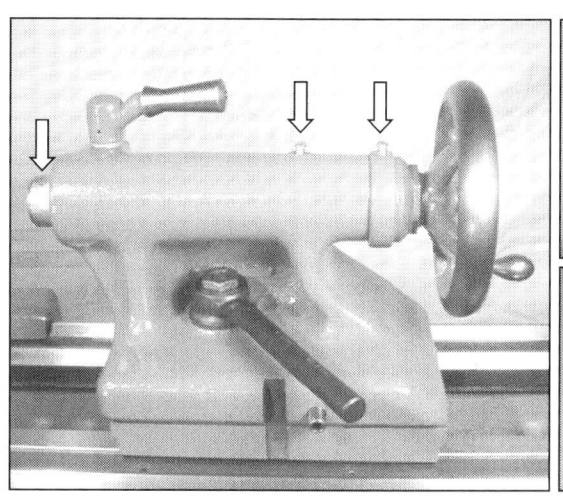
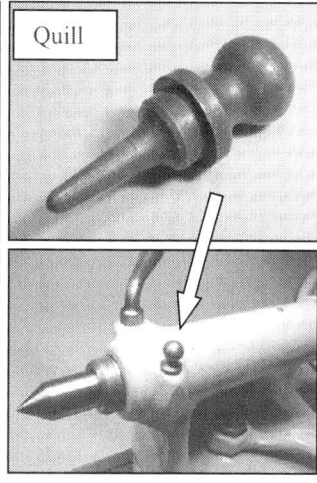

Step 4: The Tailstock

When in regular use, all tailstock oil cups should be filled with **Type C** oil daily. Note that most 9" lathes did not use oil cups so there are two oil holes; one on the top of the tailstock and one on the handwheel collar. The tailstock spindle and locking lever should also be removed, cleaned and lubricated periodically. Remove the spindle by simple turning the handwheel counter-clockwise until the spindle is fully ejected from the tailstock. Make sure to clean and re-oil the key-slot in the quill that keeps the spindle from rotating. Since the entire tailstock is easy to remove from the lathe, the bearing surfaces on the bottom of the base casting should be thoroughly cleaned and reoiled occasionally to prevent dirt and chips from becoming embedded and scoring the bed ways. For tailstocks that have a brass oil quill and a lubricant well (which was used for lubricating the tailstock dead center when turning between centers), the well should be cleaned out periodically and refilled with a small amount of oil mixed with Lubriplate 930-AA grease. The Lubriplate can be purchased in small tubes for about $5. It's interesting to note that in older publications, SBL recommended using powdered white lead mixed with machine oil "to the consistency of thick cream" for use in the quill well. Notwithstanding that fact that lead is not the safest material to handle, it did do a great job of lubricating the dead centers. Use of white lead (if you can actually find it) is not a recommended method today. Not all SBL lathes were configured with an oil quill and by the 1950's this feature was mostly gone.

Step 5: The Motor and Countershaft

Electric Motors

Originally, most electric motors supplied from the South Bend factory were of the "open drip proof" type which used plain bronze sleeve bearings (sometimes referred to as "Oilite bearings") that required regular oiling through a small port on each end of the motor housing. Open-Drip-Proof simply means the motor frame has openings that allow air (and dirt unfortunately) to circulate through the motor for cooling as opposed to motors with sealed cases that rely on an internal fan for cooling. Oil cups just like those found on the lathe were commonly used but some motors had small plugs or screws to keep contaminants out of the motor bearings. Round felt wicks were also used in many of these motors to supply oil to the bearings. To change out these felt wicks, use a small length of music wire with a hook on the end to fish the old felt out of the motor case. Reinstall the new wick by inserting, rotating and feeding the wick into the hole much like screwing in a lightbulb. Ball bearing motors were less common on older models but do exist. On most vintage ball bearing motors, grease must be injected periodically through the grease fittings in the motor housing to keep them lubricated.

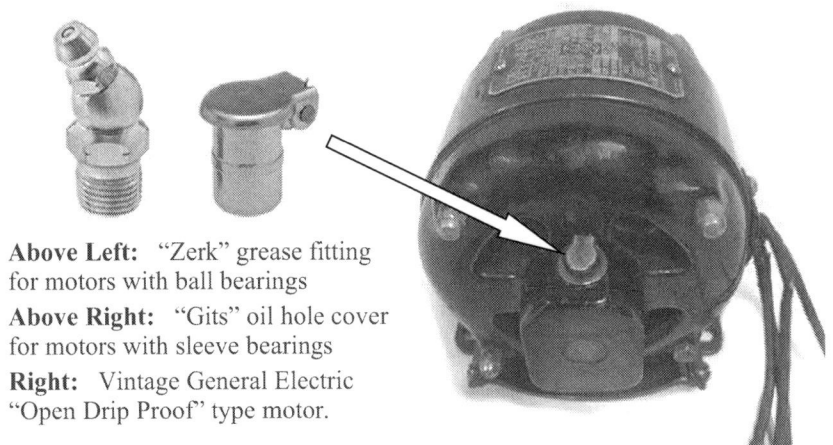

Above Left: "Zerk" grease fitting for motors with ball bearings

Above Right: "Gits" oil hole cover for motors with sleeve bearings

Right: Vintage General Electric "Open Drip Proof" type motor.

With old motors, too much lubrication of motor bearings is as bad as insufficient lubrication. Excess oil is harmful to the commutator, windings and brushes. It also causes dust to collect in the motor which may interfere with ventilation, causing the motor to overheat and burn out. Only use a few drops of **Type A** oil when lubricating.

If your lathe still has the original motor, there is no need to be overly concerned and you should not change it out just because it uses electricity and it is very old. The parts that you need to pay attention to are the wire motor leads and all connections at or leading to the motor. If the insulation on the wires is cracking or is severely frayed as is the case with most braided cloth wire, it would be wise to change out the motor. It should be noted that some older electrical cables used asbestos as a fire-proofing material in the insulation so care should be taken when working with crumbling wire insulation especially if it is powdery. If possible, keep the old motor with the lathe. It's nice to have all the original parts if they survived this long together. Frankly, there are many vintage motors out that that are still performing just fine because they were cleaned and lubricated just like the lathe. Does that sound familiar?

Electric motor technology has advanced a bit since the 1940's so with the introduction of permanently sealed ball bearings, most modern motors require no maintenance at all. If you decide to change out the motor and controls, a 1725 RPM TEFC ½ hp NEMA 56 frame motor will fit most horizontal drive benchtop lathes and a 1725 RPM ¾ hp to 1-½ hp NEMA 56 frame motor will work for most underneath drives. Other configurations are readily available.

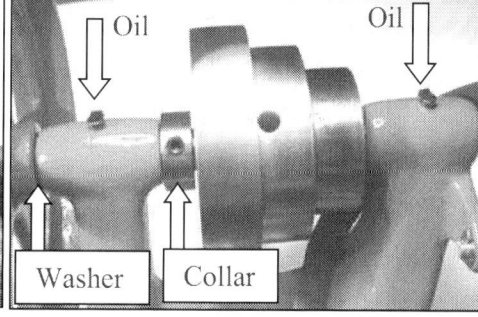

Counter-Shafts

The counter-shaft drive unit on benchtop horizontal drive lathes typically have either plain cast iron bearings on the older models or bronze sleeve bearings on later models. The two oil fill cups on top of the drive unit should be filled daily using **Type B** oil. If the drive unit leaks oil significantly on the flywheel side, check the two hard fiber washers on either side of the bearing housing; they may need to be adjusted or replaced. They are held in place by a plain collar.

Older lathes with the cast iron base have drive bearings which are lubricated by a "ring oiler" which should be checked and topped off daily. In some models, there was a small reservoir that used loose wool packing to help retain the oil around the shaft. That packing should be fished out and replaced if sludge has built up in the reservoir. The lower cone pulley shaft on later model South Bends have permanently sealed ball bearings which are packed with grease at the factory and require no further lubrication. The belt tension release lever and belt tension adjusting mechanism should be lubricated with **Type C** machine oil weekly when in normal use.

Left: Lathe with enclosed cast iron base showing all oiling ports.

Above: Permanently sealed ball bearings used on many of the later model lathes. These do require replacement if the bearing loses grease and becomes noisy.

After Oiling the Lathe, Wipe it Down

After the 5-step lubrication process is complete, the excess oil should be wiped off the non-bearing surfaces of the lathe with a clean soft cloth. If the oil is allowed to remain on painted surfaces and non-critical parts, it becomes a trap which allows dust, dirt and chips to accumulate. On older lathes, if they look particularly dirty, it is usually because of this excess oil. Well lubricated lathes will attract dirt, so dirt is not necessarily an indicator of lathe condition.

Basic Lathe Adjustments

Important Initial Adjustments

When the lathe is first set up, it is important to verify that the machine is made to operate within original specifications and that the lathe will perform properly. As designed, the lathe has a number of mechanical adjustments provided so that the performance can be "fine-tuned". Periodic inspection and adjustment will prevent poor quality work or possible damage to the machine. With experience you will learn when minor adjustments are needed but it is also important to periodically check and measure critical components.

Leveling the Lathe Bed

The lathe must be carefully leveled by using different thickness shims between the lathe feet and the floor. The lathe bed is the reference point for all leveling operations. Floors are never perfectly flat so if shims are not used, the heavy weight of the lathe may cause the bed to be twisted as the legs conform to the floor surface, which in turn will throw the headstock and tailstock out of alignment. Any misalignment will cause the lathe to turn and bore a taper. It will also cause the tailstock center point to shift as the tailstock is moved along the lathe bed, which means that constant readjustment of the tailstock set-over will be required.

If the lathe is not properly leveled it cannot turn accurately.

Shims for leveling the lathe should be made of brass or steel and large fender washers of different thicknesses work well. Wood shims should not be used since they will compress with age. When placing shims under the cabinet base at the headstock end of the lathe, use the shims only under the bolt pads. There should be a gap around the entire base except where the bolts go through the leg and into the floor. Foam weather stripping can be placed in the gap around the base to prevent chips from entering the base thereby making it easier to clean. Do not use caulk or other permanent sealing materials.

Precision Machinist Level (Starrett Model 199Z Shown above)

Use a Precision Machinist Level

A precision machinist level should be used for leveling the lathe. The level should be at least 12 inches long and sufficiently sensitive to show movement of the bubble when a .003" shim is placed under one end of it. A carpenter's level, combination square, or bullseye level should not be used for leveling because they do not have sufficient sensitivity. Precision levels are quite expensive but a good investment. Before starting the process, make sure that the bed ways are clean. Check the top of the bed ways for small burrs, and if any burrs are present remove them carefully with a fine mill file.

Precision levels require careful handling. Never hold the level with the palm of your hand over the top of the glass vial as the heat from your hand may cause the vial to distort which may affect the accuracy. After placing the level on the lathe bed, remove your hand and allow 30 seconds for the bubble to settle before taking a reading. The relative bubble position must be consistent between all readings.

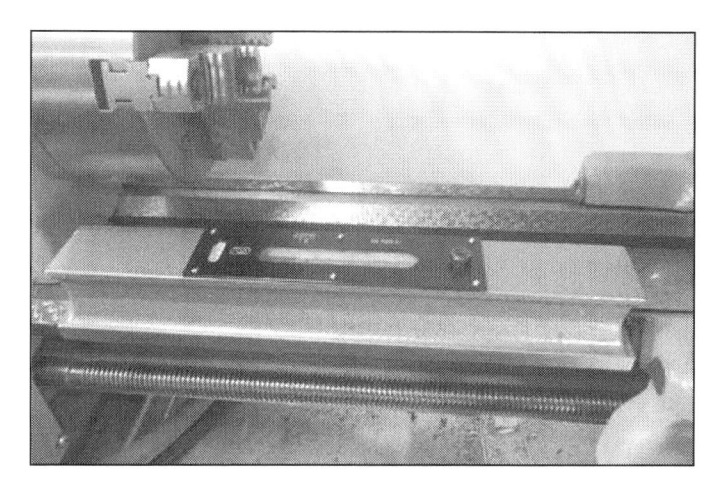

Longitudinal Leveling (Left to Right)

The lathe should first be leveled longitudinally by placing the level on the bed parallel with the ways near the center of the lathe bed. Loosen the floor bolts and shim under the lathe mounting pads until the bed is approximately level longitudinally. This leveling is not as critical since it does not affect the accuracy of the lathe.

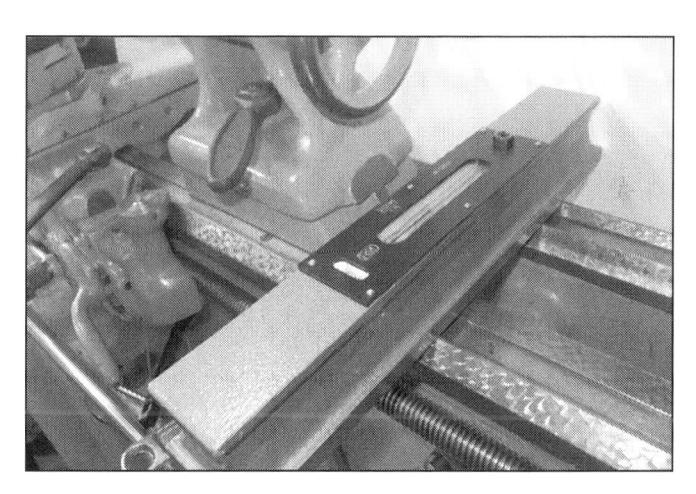

Transverse Leveling (Front to Back)

When the lathe is roughly level longitudinally, place the level across the bed ways immediately in front of the headstock, (see page 37). Allow the bubble to settle and note the position of the bubble. Without turning the level end for end, move the level to the tailstock end of the bed and repeat the reading. Place shims beneath the lathe at the points indicated by the level as being too low. Alternately check the leveling of the lathe at the headstock end and then the tailstock end and adjust the shims as needed until the lathe is perfectly level at both ends.

After the lathe has been properly leveled, carefully tighten the floor bolts uniformly so that they will have an even tension. Check the leveling of the lathe again after tightening the floor bolts and make any adjustments to the shims as needed. It will take time to do this operation properly and it can become frustrating because of the sensitivity of the level, however the extra care taken at this step will more than pay for itself with perfectly cylindrical workpieces.

Leveling Bench-Mounted Lathes

Bench mounted lathes such as the 9" workshop lathes and the 10K (Light 10) must be mounted to a heavy, rigid bench in order to perform correctly. Steel cabinet type benches can be purchased which have tops large enough to mount both the lathe and the horizontal drive unit. It is recommended that the cabinet have mounting feet that it can be fastened to the shop floor and roughly leveled before leveling the lathe. Bench lathes are leveled by placing shims between the top surface of the bench and the bottom of the lathe feet, so the bench only needs to be roughly leveled.

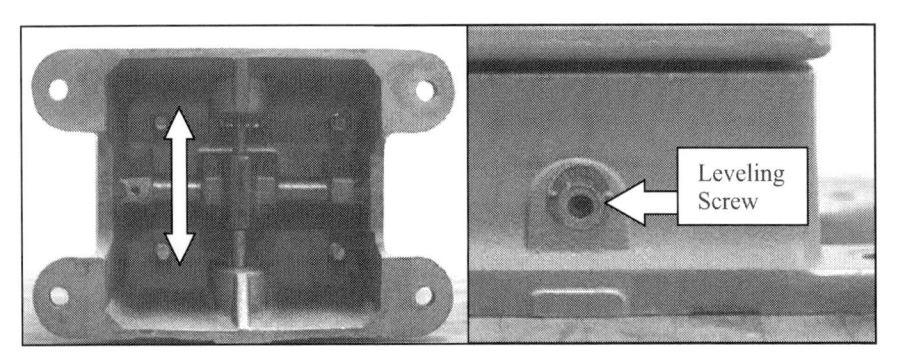

Some South Bend Lathes have leveling screws located in the front and back of the tailstock leg (see above). These screws may be used alternately for making very fine adjustments only after the course leveling of the lathe bed has been completed. The leg is on a steel pivot so the screws "tilt" the bed slightly to achieve the level. One screw must be loosened first and other tightened in the desired direction. Both screws must be tightened when leveling is complete.

A Simple Test for Checking the Level of the Lathe

There are many conditions which may alter the level of the lathe so it is important to periodically check the level. If at any time the lathe does not turn accurately (especially if it produces tapered turnings), one of the first things to check is the leveling. A simple turning test can be used to check the leveling of the lathe but it can also be used to fine tune the leveling of a lathe when a precision level is not available. Essentially this process is a poor man's level.

To test the lathe bed level, chuck a round steel bar approximately one-inch diameter in the lathe and machine two shallow collars of equal diameter about four inches apart. Then take a light cut no more than .001" to .002" in depth across both collars, using a fine feed that will not make the bar deflect under load. The setting of the cross feed should not be altered while taking the final cut across the two collars. A slow spindle speed should be used to reduce the chance of the bar whipping since it cannot be supported by the tailstock.

After completing both cuts in one pass, wipe off the test bar to remove any turning residue. Carefully measure the diameter of both collars with a micrometer. If they are exactly equal the lathe is level. "Equal" is generally within about a .0002" range for a standard thimble micrometer. Greater accuracy is possible with a friction thimble micrometer since the force applied to the thimble is constant during measurement. A taper indicated by unequal collar diameters means that the lathe is not level and that the cutting tool is not traveling perfectly parallel to the center axis of the work. If the diameter of the collar nearest the tailstock is greater than that of the collar nearest the headstock, shim under the front of the tailstock leg until both collars turn equal. If the diameter of the collar nearest the headstock is greater than that of the tailstock collar, shim under the rear tailstock leg until both collars turn to the same diameter.

Adjusting the Lathe to the Operator

Fitting the workplace and machines to the human (ergonomics) was not often considered 75 years ago. Over the years however, the machine-operator interface to become safer and more efficient. We have options today that did not exist in the 1940's. For instance, lathe benches were one height; 29-¼" inches so if the operator was short, the work was positioned too high. If the operator was tall, then the work was too low and they had to lean over the work all day. Regarding safety, chip shields, belt guards and gear covers were almost never installed on lathes in the 1940's and it was sufficient to tell the operator "do not put your hand in the moving gears". We all know how that would turn out today. Considering that these lathes were built in a different era means that contemporary operators must be aware of the dangers and take steps to prevent injury. Heavy adjustable-height benches are available now which can set the machine to the user's height. Ring lamps can be mounted to the lathe bench and used as both a chip guard and work lighting. Aftermarket belt guards can be installed; low voltage variable speed motor drives can be used in place of open drives; vacuum chip removal instead of sweeping makes cleaning and operation safer.

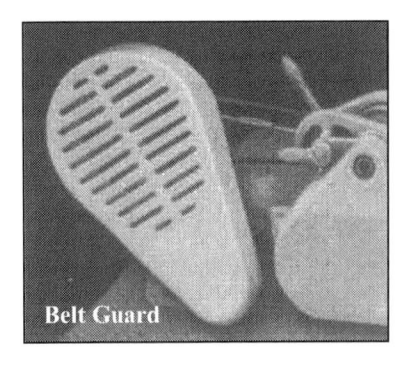

Adjusting the Belt Tensions

Counter-
Shaft
Cone
Pulley

Motor
V-Belts

V-Belt
Adjust-
ment

Cone
Pulley
Belt

Belt
Tension
Release
Lever

Cone
Pulley
Belt
Adjust-
ment

In order to transmit adequate power from the motor to the lathe spindle, all belts must be properly adjusted. If any belt is too loose it will slip, and if it is too tight it will cause loss of power through the additional friction in the bearing, and it may actually cause excessive wear on the machine. Properly adjusted, the belt should be just tight enough to transmit sufficient power without slipping. Belt material is also important. The original flat leather belts that SBL used for all of the cone pulleys were adequate, however they often stretched easily and were susceptible to retaining oil and other contaminants. There are newer alternatives that provide much better service. Flat urethane belts or rubber belts with a nylon core work best for the 10" to 16" lathes where the belt must be spliced and glued (or welded in the case of the urethane belts). For all 9" and 10K horizontal drive

Lathes it is possible to remove the spindle and drive shaft pulley easily, so an endless serpentine automotive belt is a cheap and reliable alternative to leather and there is no splicing.

When replacing a belt, it is often easier to order the belt already sized and the ends skived (meaning tapered on the ends so that it is ready for gluing). Typical belt sizes for most SBL's are shown in the table below however you will need to confirm the actual size required for your lathe before ordering. A flexible metal tape measure works well if you place the numbered face of the tape against the pulley so that it flexes more easily as you wrap it around the pulley. Simply mark the back of the tape and flip it over to read the measurement. Make sure when measuring for the new belt that the belt tension adjuster is approximately centered so that there is sufficient room to adjust in either direction once the belt is installed.

South Bend Lathe Drive Belt Lengths and Widths				
Lathe Model	Thickness (Inches)	Width (In. +/- 1/16")	Length (Inches)	Original Part Number
9" Horizontal Drive Unit	9/64	3/4	53-1/2	PT2223N4
9" Underdrive Metal Bench	9/64	3/4	61	P12200N3
10K Horizontal Drive Unit	9/64	3/4	50-1/4	PT2226K4
10K Underdrive Cabinet Metal Bench	9/64	3/4	61-7/8	PT2208K3
10" Underdrive Cabinet Metal Bench	5/32	1	58-1/8	PT2201R3
10" Underdrive Cabinet Leg Floor	5/32	1	61-1/2	PT2202R3
13" Underdrive Cabinet Leg Floor (3 step cone)	5/32	2	61-1/2	PT2195T3
13" Underdrive Cabinet Leg Floor (4 step cone)	5/32	1-1/2	61-1/2	PT2203T3
14-1/2" Underdrive Cabinet Leg Floor (3 step cone)	5/32	2-1/2	64-5/8	PT2196F3
14-1/2" Underdrive Cabinet Leg Floor (4 step cone)	5/32	1-1/2	64-1/2	PT2204F3
16" Underdrive Cabinet Leg Floor (4 step cone)	5/32	2	68-1/4	PT2205H3
16" Underdrive Cabinet Leg Floor (3 step cone)	5/32	2-1/2	68-1/4	PT2207H3
16"/24" Underdrive Cabinet Leg Floor (3 step cone)	5/32	2-1/2	77-1/2	PT2197V2
16"/24" Underdrive Cabinet Leg Floor (4 step cone)	5/32	2	76-3/8	PT2206H3

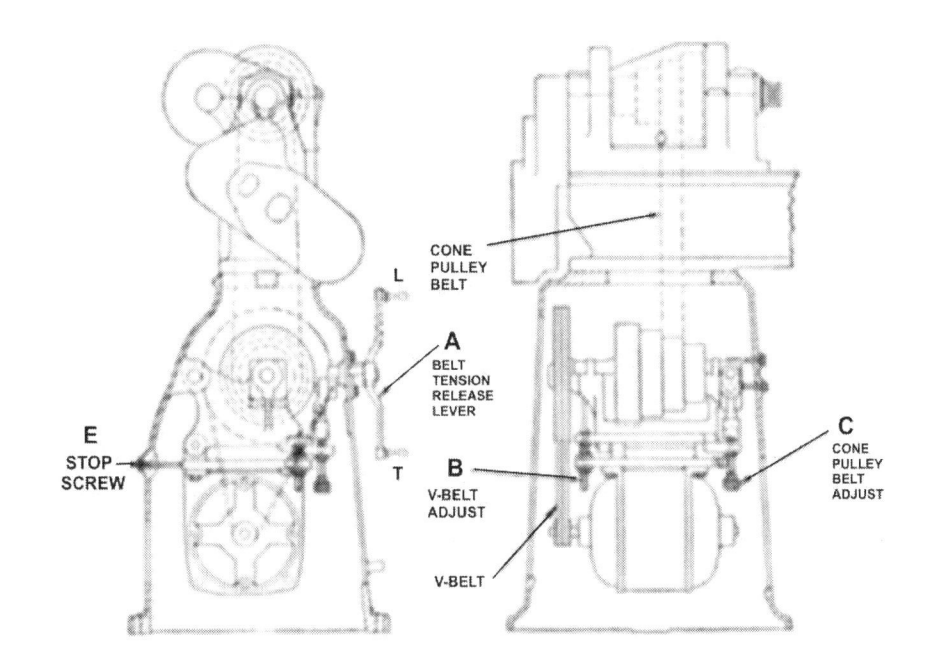

13" Underneath Drive Showing V-Belt
and Cone Pulley Belt Adjustments

Adjusting the Motor "V" Belt

The adjustment of the V-belts which transmit power from the motor to the countershaft pulley can be tested easily by pressing on the belts mid-way between the pulleys with one finger. It should be possible to deflect the belts about ¾" with moderate force.

On 10" and Larger Lathes, the V-belts are adjusted by turning the adjusting nuts on screw "B". Turning these nuts to the left tightens the belt. If the lathe has a stop screw "E", this screw must be loosened by several revolutions before adjusting the V-belt tension. After the correct belt tension is secured, stop screw "E" should be readjusted so that it supports the weight of the motor drive mechanism and eliminates play when the belt tension release lever "A" is in the lower position "T". Later model lathes have a counterbalance spring which eliminates the need for the stop screw.

Rotate Turnbuckle to Increase / Decrease Tension

X CONE PULLEY BELT ADJUST

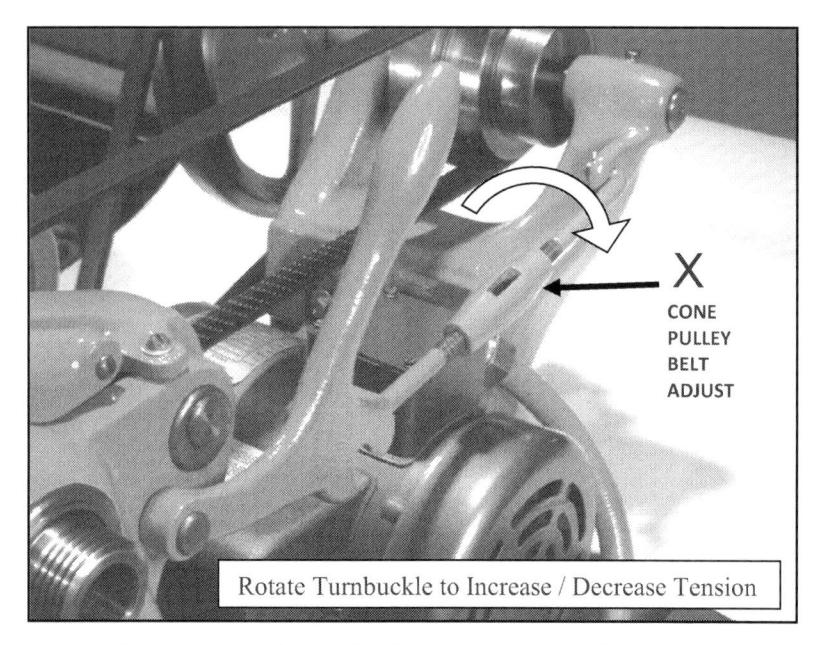

On the 9" or 10K lathes with horizontal or underneath drives (see diagrams on the next page), the V-belt tension is adjusted by loosening the 4 bolts on the motor base "O", and then sliding the motor up or down to achieve the desired tension. Make sure the faces of the motor and driven pulleys are parallel and that the motor is not tilted before re-securing the motor bolts.

When dual V-belts are replaced, a "Matched Set" of new belts should be installed. Both belts must be exactly the same length, otherwise they will not perform correctly.

Adjusting the Cone Pulley Belt

The tension of the flat cone pulley belt can be tested by pressing on the belt between the pulleys with one finger. It should be possible to depress the belt about ½" at a point 4" to 6" from the headstock cone pulley. The belt should be just tight enough to run under load without slipping.

On 9" Underdrive Lathes, the cone pulley belt tension is adjusted by turning turnbuckle "X" in the diagram. This adjustment should be made with the belt tension release lever "A" locked into position "T". Horizontal Drive lathes work the same way but lever A is on top of the lathe as shown in the photograph above.

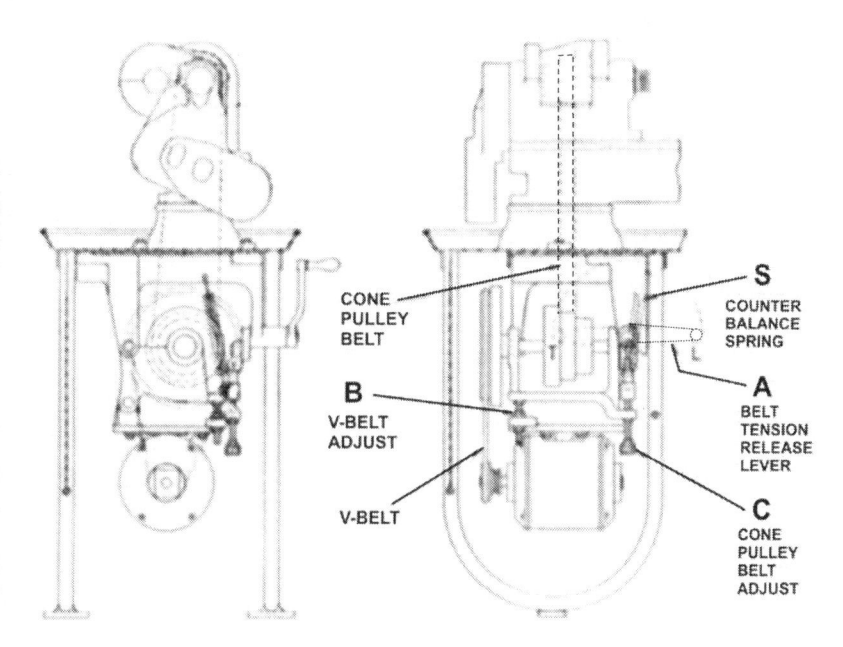

Belt tension adjustments on 10" Bench Lathes

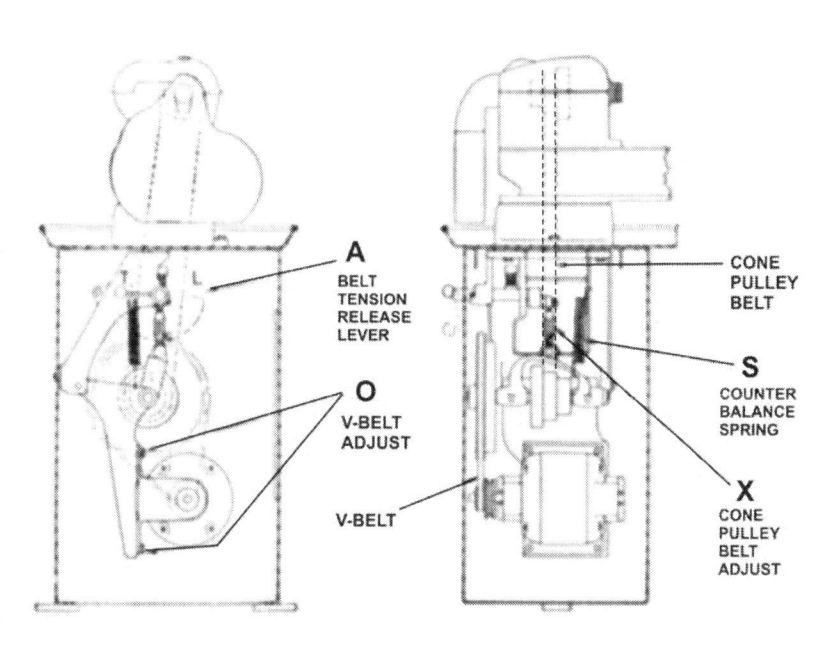

Belt tension adjustments on 9" Lathes

On 10" and larger Industrial Lathes, the cone pulley belt tension is adjusted by turning the knurled knob "C". This adjustment should be made with the belt tension release lever "A" in the position "T". Turning this knob clockwise tightens the belt. If the lathe has a stop screw E this screw must be unscrewed several revolutions before adjusting the cone pulley belt tension or it will not be possible to move the carriage.

After adjusting the cone pulley belt, stop screw "E" must be tightened so that will support the weight of the motor drive unit and eliminate play when the belt tension release lever "A" is in the lower position "T". Note: Stop screw "E" is not used on later model lathes.

Splicing Belts

The flat belts used on most underdrive and industrial model lathes must be spliced and rejoined since an endless belt cannot be installed through the bed and headstock without cutting it first.

When using leather or reinforced rubber-faced belts, the splicing is generally done by "skiving" the joint first. Skiving tapers the ends of the belt so that they overlap with a large surface area. The two surfaces are then glued and clamped together to form an endless belt.

When using Urethane belting, the splice is a butt joint which is welded together using an electric hot knife which is held in close proximity to the joint surfaces. Once the melting point is reached, the ends are aligned and forced together until cooled. Trimming the "mushroom" after welding is necessary for smooth running.

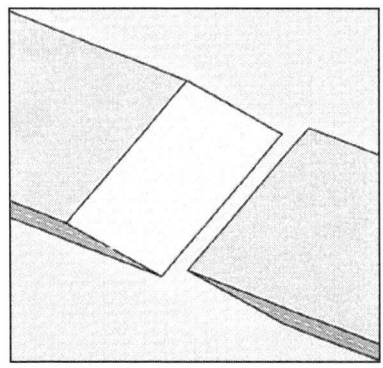

Above: Skived joint used for leather and reinforced rubber belts

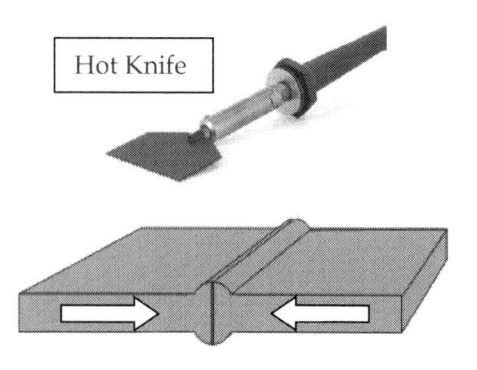

Above: Electric "Hot Knife" used for butt-welding Urethane belts. Note the "mushroom"

Adjusting the Take-up Washer or Bearing

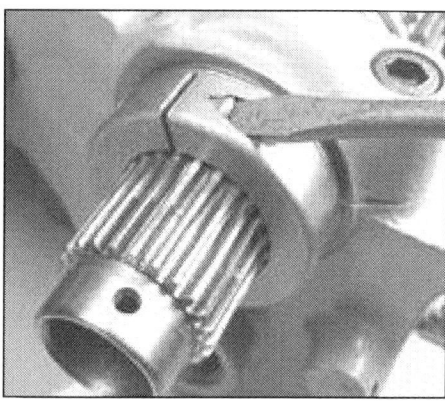

Take-up Nut & Washer

The take-up washer is located on the tail of the spindle. The purpose of this washer is to remove excessive lateral play in the spindle (this is the slight left to right movement in the spindle when viewed from the front of the lathe). The take-up washer is typically made of a red hard fiber material and contains a fixed brass stud to allow the take-up nut and washer to rotate together when the spindle is in motion. Lubrication for the face of the washer which is in contact with the headstock casting comes from the left spindle bearing. The design is such that some clearance between the washer and headstock is necessary, otherwise there will be no room for the oil and the washer will wear out prematurely.

It is advisable to periodically remove the take-up washer for cleaning and inspection but this does not require regular attention. To remove the washer, remove the reversing gear bracket, loosen the slotted locking screw on the take-up collar and unscrew both the collar & take-up washer from the spindle by holding the spindle and turning the collar counter-clockwise. Clean the bearing face on the headstock, then clean the take-up washer and nut. Make sure the washer is not cracked or degraded. Lightly oil the washer with Type A spindle oil, align the brass stud on the washer with the recess in the take-up collar and then thread the two onto the spindle and snug it up against the headstock bearing face (finger tight only). Back off the collar approximately 1/12 turn counter-clockwise in order to provide clearance for lubrication and then tighten the collar locking screw. There should be approximately .001" end-play in the spindle and it should spin easily by hand. If the spindle does not spin easily, back off the collar slightly until movement is satisfactory.

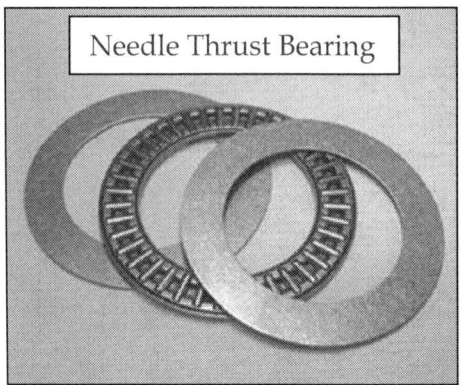

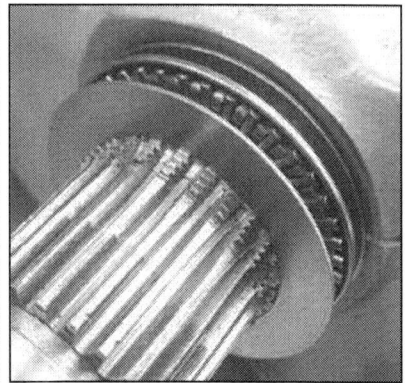

Needle Thrust Bearing

Replacement of the Take-up Washer

Often the take-up washer is missing on older lathes, or it has become damaged through poor adjustment, or has simply degraded over time and is no longer usable. Note that later model 10"-16" lathes were equipped with a thrust ball bearing in place of the take-up washer so this step is not needed. Options for replacement:

Option 1 for all model lathes: Turn a new take-up washer out of a high strength polymer material such as Delrin. Delrin is readily available, easy to machine, has very good low-friction properties and is very durable for this application. The washer can be made slightly thicker than the original without interfering with the reversing lever bracket. For installing a new brass stud, countersink a hole in the washer, turn a new shouldered stud that fits the smaller diameter of the countersunk hole. Insert the stud and peen over or "mushroom" the brass head on the opposite side to secure it in the washer recess.

Option 2 for 9" and 10k lathes: A quicker and much easier option is to use a standard needle thrust bearing. These bearings are very thin and can easily replace the take-up washer on 9" and 10k lathe. The bearing consists of a caged row of needle bearings sandwiched between two thrust washers (see above). The installation method is the same as for the original washer except that it does need to be regularly cleaned and lubricated with **Type A** spindle oil. Small chips or dirt that enters this type of bearing will cause chattering.

Adjusting the Back Gear

The back-gears on the lathe headstock are held in position by friction bushings located in the headstock. The style and adjustment methods are dictated by the model of the lathe.

For all 9" and 10k Lathes (see photos below): First engage the back-gears using the eccentric shaft lever and allow the mating gears to bottom out. Back off the eccentric lever until you feel a slight rock between mating gears when the back gear is rotated. Tighten the slotted set screw and jam nut beneath the eccentric lever. Tighten the square head set screw against the internal spring to put enough tension on the bushing so that gears will be held in mesh on heavy cuts, but not so tight that the eccentric shaft lever is hard to operate. Make the final adjustment by allowing the lathe to run for a few minutes. If there is an abnormal amount of gear rattling noise, the gear clearance is too great. Adjust by slightly unscrewing the slotted set screw (to bring the gears closer together) and testing for noise again. If the gears produce a growling noise, the gear clearance is too low. Adjust by turning the slotted set screw clockwise (to push the gears further apart) and then tighten the jam nut. If the gears pop out of engagement during operation or heavy cuts, you can increase the tension on the shaft by further tightening the square head set screw.

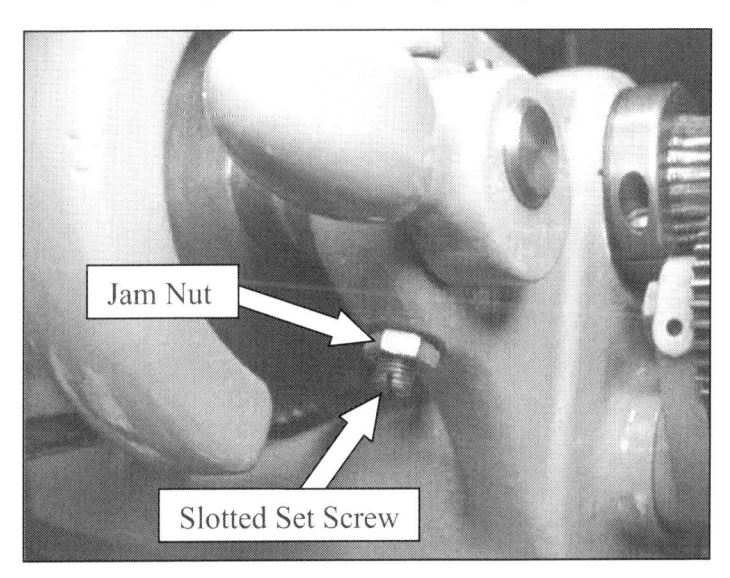

Setting the Gear Clearances on the 9" & 10K

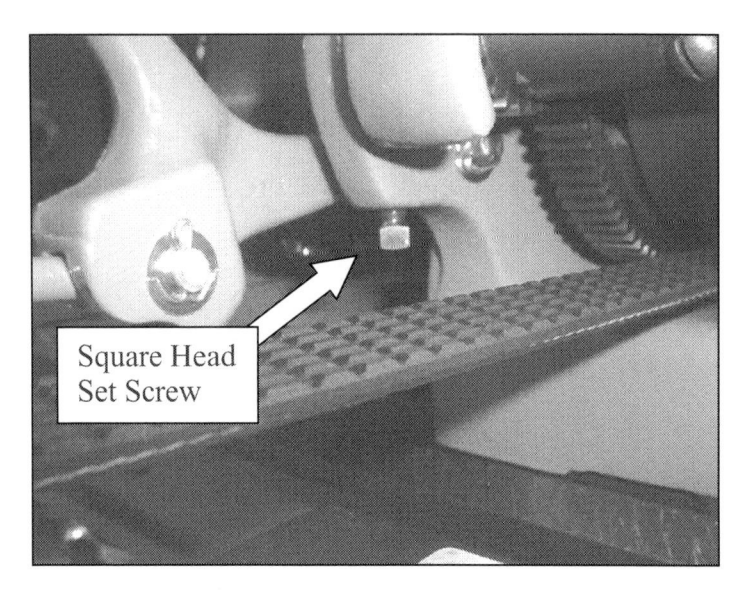

Setting the Back Gear Tension on the 9" and 10K

For Model 10L & 14-½" Lathes (see photos below): On 10L and 14-½ lathes the adjustment method is very similar. If there is significant gear rattling noise during operation, the gear clearance is too great. Adjust by slightly unscrewing the slotted set screw (to bring the gears closer together) and test it again. If the gears produce a growling noise, the gear clearance is too low. Adjust by turning the slotted set screw clockwise (to push the gears apart) and then tighten the jam nut. If the gears pop out of engagement during operation or heavy cuts, increase the tension.

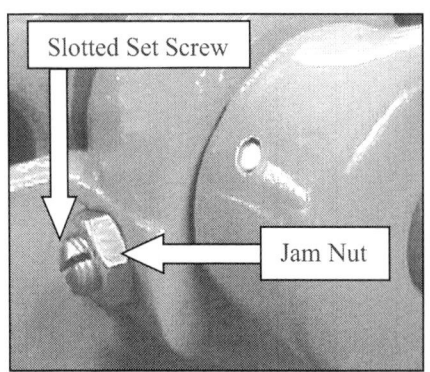

Setting the Gear Clearances   Setting the Bushing Tension

For all 13" & 16" Lathes (see photos below): On the 13" and 16" lathes, the gear depth is set at the factory by the position of the eccentric lever against a hard stop on the corresponding bushing. The bushing has a countersunk hole on the outer diameter and when this is properly aligned and fixed in place with the pointed set screw in the headstock casting, the gear depths should be properly adjusted.

The Back Gear Tension is adjustable by tightening the split bushing on the other end of the shaft. As before, if the gears pop out of engagement during operation or heavy cuts, increase the tension screw in order the clamp down more tightly on the eccentric shaft.

Back Gear on 13" & 16" Lathes: Note the design difference for setting gear depths.

Spindle Bearings

The spindle bearings on South Bend Lathes were carefully fitted when they left the factory and if the lathe was properly lubricated and maintained, adjustment is usually not necessary, even after many years. The spindle bearing clearances should be tested before any adjustment is considered. Do not assume that the bearings are too tight because they heat up. As pointed out earlier, the heating may be caused by the lack of oil, dirty oil or the wrong type of oil. Chatter is not necessarily an indication that spindle clearances are too loose. Chatter may actually be caused by bearings that are too tight. Check that the headstock bearing cap bolts are not loose and tighten them if necessary. Tight means approximately 25 lbs. of force on a standard 6" Allen Wrench.

In summary: Consider every other possible cause BEFORE adjusting the spindle bearing clearances.

If it is possible that adjustment is required, then the amount of the adjustment needs to be determined through testing before the bearing caps are disturbed, otherwise there is no reference point. Do not remove the bearing caps or loosen any screws until the bearing clearance is tested. The adjustment of the spindle bearings is critical, and incorrect adjustment can damage the lathe.

Before testing the spindle bearings, release the tension on the flat cone pulley belt. Make sure that the lathe is properly leveled and a that it is securely bolted to the floor or workbench.

Make Sure Bearing Cap Bolts are Tight Before Testing!

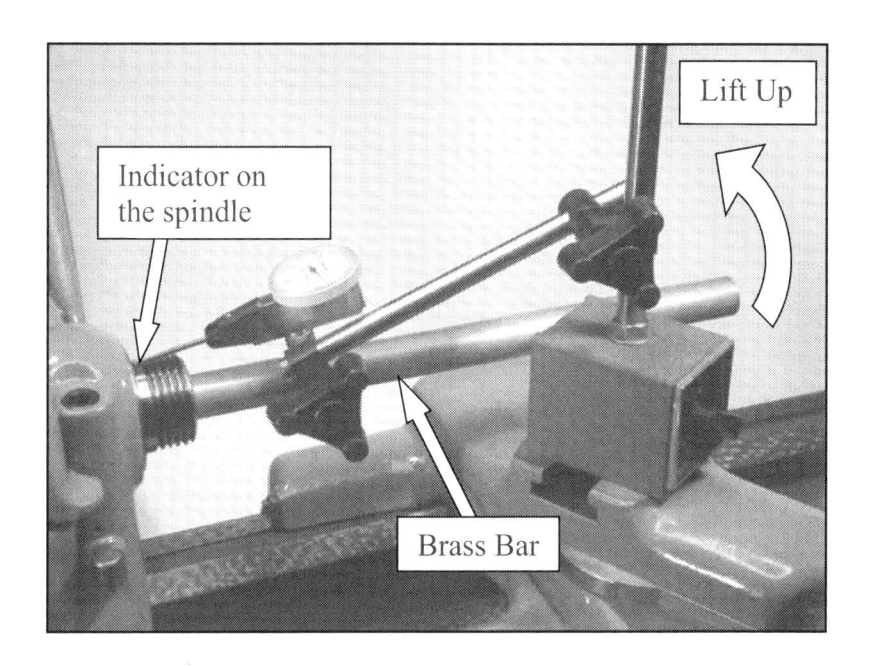

Testing the Spindle Bearings

Mount the base of a dial test indicator on the top of the lathe compound with the tip of the indicator contacting the top of the spindle nearest the smooth collar. Place a 2 ft. long by ¾" diameter brass bar (or similar soft metal) through the spindle. Push down on the bar lightly (approximately 5 lbs. force) to displace the oil film on the bottom of the spindle and then zero the indicator. Lift up on the bar with approximately 75 lbs. of force and note the change in the indicator reading. Acceptable readings per the original SBL Specs:

All Lathes (Cast Iron Plain Bearings): .001" - .002"

All Lathes (Bronze Shell Bearings): .0007" - .0010"

Any indicator reading outside these ranges may indicate that bearing adjustment is necessary. On any old machinery there always is a risk to disturbing the bearings that measure on the high side of the specification (loose), so it is recommended that you consider that risk compared to any small difference in the measured reading. For instance, if a 13" lathe with bronze bearings measured .0012" on the indicator, it would not be wise to take the caps off and attempt to compensate for a .0002" difference. There is that much error in the measurement alone. *If it is very close, leave it alone.*

Adjusting the Spindle Bearings

In the event adjustment is needed, laminated shims are provided under the bearing caps for adjusting the spindle bearings on all South Bend Lathes. Each lamination removed will reduce the bearing clearance. In addition to the laminated shims, thin .001" shims are included on most 10" and larger lathes with bronze spindle bearings.

When removing the headstock bearing caps or working with the spindle at any time, extreme care should be used. Before removing the bearing caps or shims, thoroughly clean the headstock using a brush and vacuum to remove all contaminants from the area. Wipe down the area with a clean lint-free cloth. Be especially diligent in cleaning the area around the bearing caps and in the screw recesses or slots. Do not allow even the smallest dirt particle, chip or any other foreign material get into the bearing or the space between the bearing cap and the bearing shell. Shims, screws and the threaded holes in the cap should also be thoroughly cleaned after removal.

When adjusting the bearing clearance on 10" and larger lathes which have the removable bearing caps, it is extremely important that the total thickness of shim stack on either side of the bearing cap be kept the same within .001". If the difference in height is greater than .001", the bearing cap will not be pulled down evenly and may be forced out of round. Note that 9" and 10k lathes do not have removable bearing caps so this is not applicable. Number the shims with a felt-tip marker and note the location during removal so that they can be reinstalled in the same position and in the same order.

For all 9" and 10k lathes

The laminated shims can be a bit hard to remove because of the paint that is usually covering the shim slot. Scrape the paint from the shim slot. Remove the bearing cap bolt and the shim lamination stack from the head. Be careful not to scratch the spindle when removing the shims. Do not use a screwdriver or other steel tool. Use a piece of thin brass bar stock approximately the same thickness as the slot and use it to lightly tap the shims from the slot. Measure the original thickness of the shim stack and then remove one of the .002" layers. If the clearance is too loose, cut a new shim from stock that is approximately 0.0010" to 0.0015" in thickness to match the

> Shim Slot

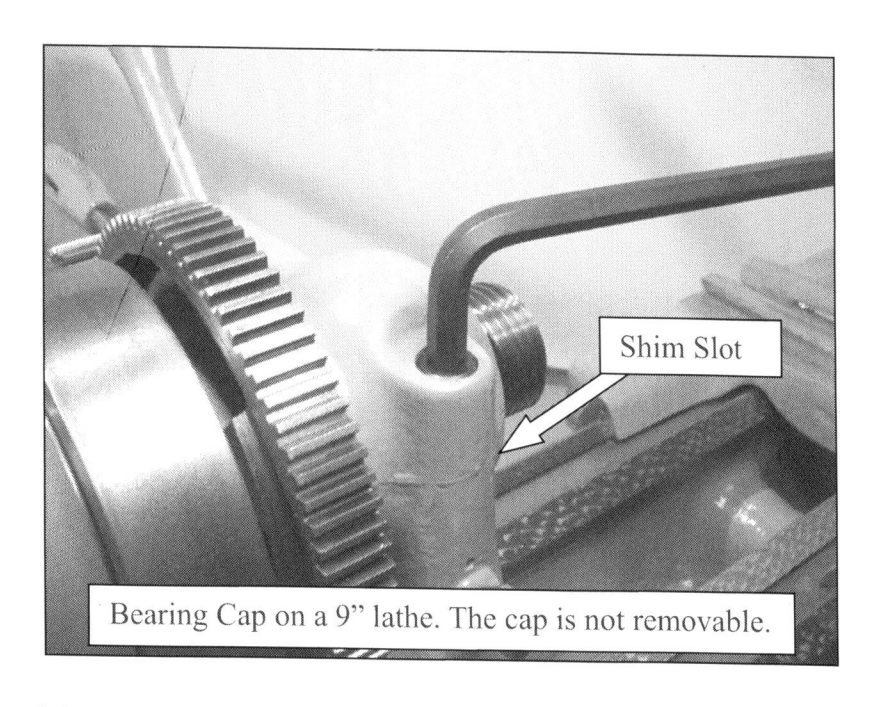

Bearing Cap on a 9" lathe. The cap is not removable.

original shim profile and then insert it into the stack in place of the original .002" shim. This is a net reduction in total shim height of .001 to .0005 depending on the amount of adjustment needed. If the clearance is too tight, add a shim to the stack. Check the thickness of the total shim stack with a micrometer then reinsert the stack of shims back into the headstock. Install the bolt, retighten it and measure the clearance again. Do not allow the indicated clearance to drop below the minimum values above or there could be issues with proper lubrication of the spindle and overheating may occur. The minimum clearance specification is necessary to maintain the oil film that protects the spindle bearing surfaces, so a clearance on the higher end of the spec is actually better for the lathe than too little clearance since the lack of clearance can starve the spindle of oil and damage the bearings or spindle.

Repeat this same test procedure on the other end of the spindle by clamping the dial indicator on the headstock casting or the back-gear shroud and placing the indicator contact on the smooth outer collar of the spindle. Specifications are the same for either of the spindle bearings. Minor differences in bearing clearances between the two spindles bearings is not significant. *If it is very close, leave it alone.*

For all 10" through 16" Lathes:

If the clearance is outside of the test ranges above, then a .0015" brass shim must be added (under .0007") or removed (over .0010") from *ONE SIDE* of the bearing cap only. All shims should be made of .0015" thick brass. Remove the locking screws first and then the bearing cap bolts as shown in the original SBL machine tag below.

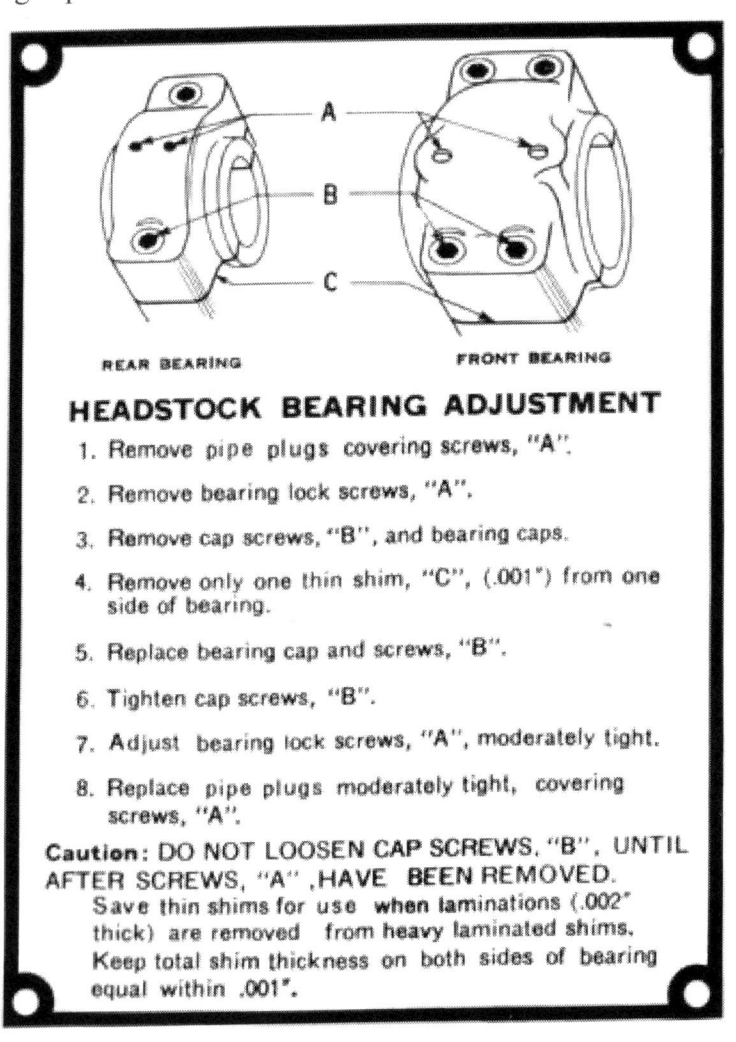

REAR BEARING   **FRONT BEARING**

HEADSTOCK BEARING ADJUSTMENT

1. Remove pipe plugs covering screws, "A".
2. Remove bearing lock screws, "A".
3. Remove cap screws, "B", and bearing caps.
4. Remove only one thin shim, "C", (.001") from one side of bearing.
5. Replace bearing cap and screws, "B".
6. Tighten cap screws, "B".
7. Adjust bearing lock screws, "A", moderately tight.
8. Replace pipe plugs moderately tight, covering screws, "A".

Caution: DO NOT LOOSEN CAP SCREWS, "B", UNTIL AFTER SCREWS, "A", HAVE BEEN REMOVED.
Save thin shims for use when laminations (.002" thick) are removed from heavy laminated shims. Keep total shim thickness on both sides of bearing equal within .001".

Remove the shim stack and measure the total thickness with a micrometer and then add or remove one .0015" shim. Cut any new brass shim to match the original profile and insert it into the stack. Check the total stack thickness of the shims before re-installing.

Install the cap bolts and tighten, then the locking screws and tighten. The locking screws act on a bronze dovetail gib that mates with the bronze bearing shell and expands the bearing inside the cap; locking it in place. Measure the bearing clearance once again. Do not allow the indicated clearance to go below the minimum values listed or there will be insufficient clearance for proper spindle lubrication. The minimum clearance specified is necessary to maintain the oil film that protects the spindle bearing surfaces, so a clearance on the high side of the specification is better than too little clearance since low clearance can starve the spindle of oil and damage the bearings. Repeat the test procedure on the other end of the spindle by clamping the dial indicator on the headstock casting and placing the indicator contact on the outer collar of the spindle.

Above: Bearing caps and brass shims used on lathes with split bronze spindle bearings.

Left: Close-up view of the bronze bearing and expander wedge with the bearing cap removed.

Adjusting the Cross Slide and Compound Gibs

South Bend Lathes are designed with dovetails on both the compound slide and cross slide which have either straight gibs or tapered gibs depending on the lathe model. The gibs can be adjusted to compensate for wear and to fine tune the slide movement. The gibs should be tight enough to eliminate play, but not tight enough to bind the slide and make the ball crank handles difficult to operate.

For Straight Gibs: Adjust the gib by cranking the slide back & forth by hand and tightening each gib screw until the slide just begins to drag, then back off 1/12 of a turn. Move to the next screw and repeat. Adjust each screw uniformly until slide movement is smooth but firm. A very light touch is required to set properly.

For Tapered Gibs: Tapered gibs are adjusted by turning the captive gib shoulder screw in or out to set the drag. Before making this adjustment, the locking set screw must be loosened at least one revolution. After adjustment, retighten the locking set screw lightly to avoid damage to the brass shoe inside or the gib screw threads.

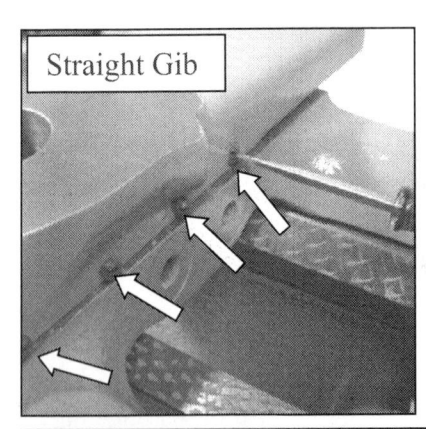

Above Left: Straight gib shown on cross slide.

Above Right: Close-up view of a tapered gib and the locking set screw.

Left: Straight gib shown on the compound slide.

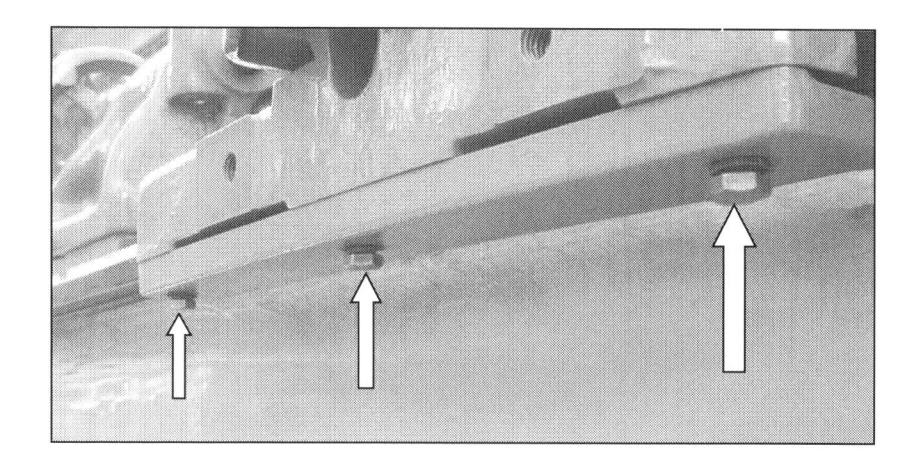

Adjusting the Saddle Gib Plate

The purpose of the saddle hold-down gib plate (see photo above) is to secure the back of the saddle to the lathe bed and prevent it from lifting during operation. Adjustment of this plate is particularly important if using a production cross slide with a rear facing tool post and inverted tool bit. The forces from turning will cause the saddle to lift and chatter if not adjusted properly. The gib plate should only be tight enough to eliminate any excess play, but not be tight enough to bind and make the carriage difficult to traverse along the lathe bed when the apron handwheel is turned.

Before adjusting, thoroughly clean the bottom side of the lathe bed and lubricate with **Type C** oil. Make sure the lock-washers are installed between the hex head bolts and the gib plate, otherwise the plate will come loose during use. Adjust the gib plate by tightening each hex head bolt sequentially against the plate while traversing the carriage. As the apron handwheel is rotated and the carriage starts to drag, back off the bolt 1/12 turn and move to the next bolt. Continue tightening uniformly across all 3 bolts until the operation is smooth and without vertical play.

Adjusting the Tailstock Set-over

Tailstock "Set-Over" is simply an adjustment mechanism by which the body of the tailstock can be moved perpendicular to the bed V-ways and then locked into place for turning tapers.

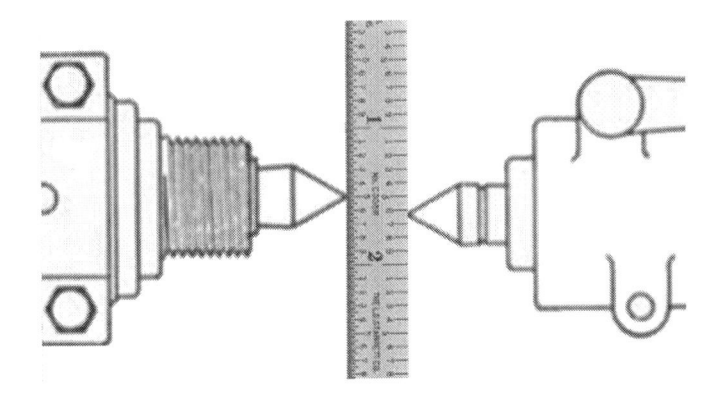

Diagram illustrating tailstock "Set-over" as viewed from above the lathe.

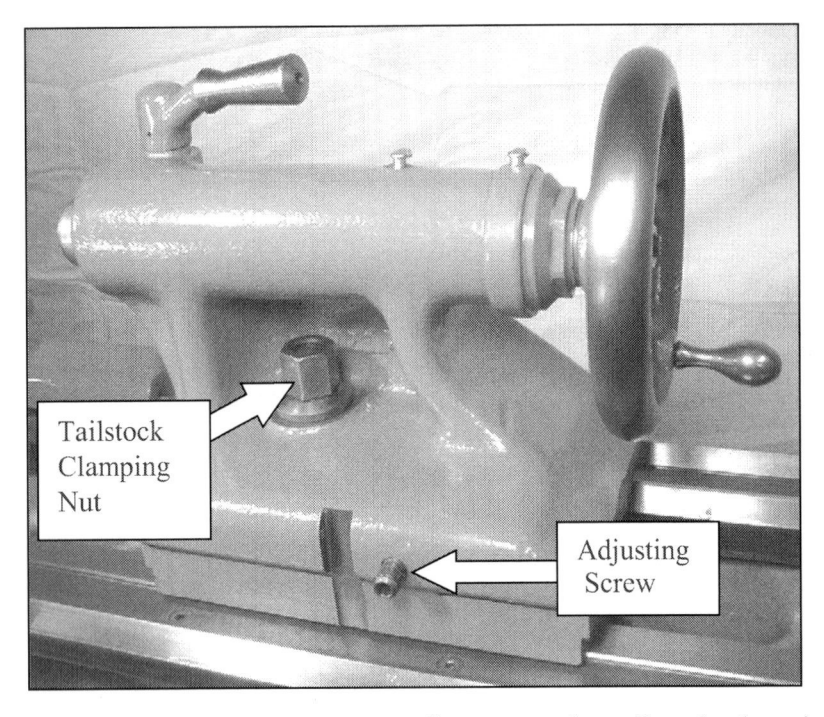

Tailstock Clamping Nut

Adjusting Screw

    In order to make the set-over adjustment, the tailstock clamping nut must be loosened first. There are two set-over adjusting screws; one on the front of the tailstock and one on the rear. The set-over is achieved by releasing one of the two set-over adjusting screws and then tightening the opposite screw. There are witness marks stamped on the end of the tail stock to show the relative position of the tailstock body to the base. These marks are for rough setting only.

Witness Marks Aligned

Witness Marks Offset

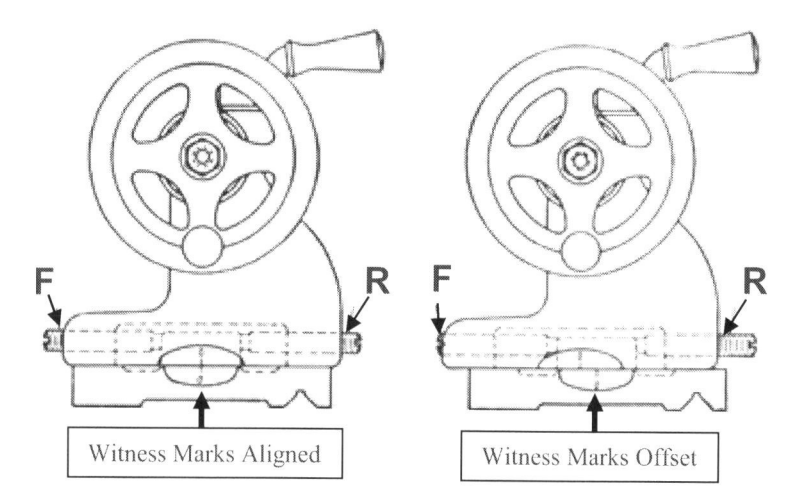

The tailstock set-over screws Front "F" and Rear "R" and witness marks are shown above. Recalling the discussion earlier on worn lathe beds, if the bed is worn in the center, this adjustment must be made depending on the length of the work. Setting the tailstock set-over on the unworn section will be different than the worn section.

Lathe Centering Buttons used with a micrometer to precisely measure the tailstock alignment.

Measuring the Tailstock Set-over

To measure the approximate tailstock set-over, a machinist's scale can be used with both edges between the two centers, as shown on the previous page. A more accurate method of determining the tailstock to headstock center alignment is to use a pair of lathe centering buttons and a micrometer. The buttons are generally 0.9" in diameter and have a center-drilled recesses on one side of the button and a flat polished surface on the other. The buttons are used in pairs by placing the them face to face between the dead centers in the headstock and tailstock. Extending the quill on the tailstock will clamp the buttons together and bring the polished faces of the buttons into contact. Once the button faces are in firm contact, the tailstock quill is locked and a micrometer is used across the interface of the two buttons to determine the accuracy of the alignment. The two faces of the micrometer spindles must bridge both buttons and the micrometer body must be held perpendicular to the lathe turning axis to get an accurate reading. Since both buttons are exactly 0.900" in diameter, a reading of exactly 0.900" on the micrometer means that the centers are aligned exactly. If one of the buttons is slightly offset and the micrometer reads 0.905" then it would mean that the tailstock center is out of alignment by .005". Highly precise positioning of the tailstock can be achieved using the alignment buttons. Buttons can be easily made or can be purchased from www.Brownells.com

The advantage of lathe centering buttons is that the vertical as well as the lateral alignment can be checked in one set-up. Just move the micrometer to the vertical axis and the height alignment can be measured as well. There is no mechanism for changing the height alignment and on older lathes with worn beds, the tailstock will often be lower than headstock center. The only way to correct vertical offset is to use thin brass shims between the tailstock body and the tailstock base. Use two shim strips with one on the quill end and one on the handwheel end to keep the tailstock level.

Left: Tailstock base with top removed. Dotted white lines represent location to shim if the tailstock center is too low due to wear on the lathe bed. Shims strips should be equal thickness.

Reference Materials

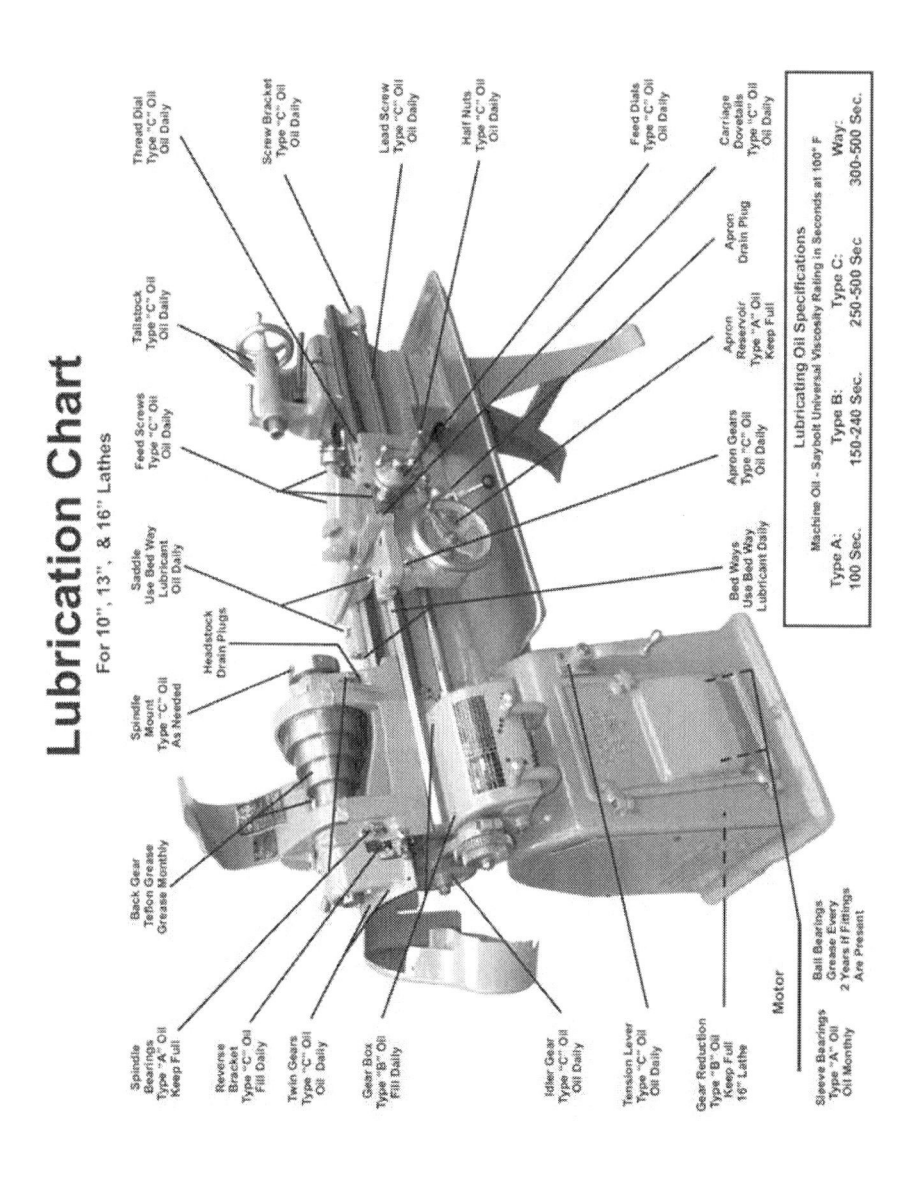

Lubrication Chart
For 10", 13", & 16" Lathes

Thread Dial — Type "C" Oil, Oil Daily
Screw Bracket — Type "C" Oil, Oil Daily
Lead Screw — Type "C" Oil, Oil Daily
Half Nuts — Type "C" Oil, Oil Daily
Feed Dials — Type "C" Oil, Oil Daily
Carriage Dovetails — Type "C" Oil, Oil Daily
Apron Drain Plug
Apron Reservoir — Type "A" Oil, Keep Full
Apron Gears — Type "C" Oil, Oil Daily
Bed Ways — Use Bed Way Lubricant Daily
Tailstock — Type "C" Oil, Oil Daily
Feed Screws — Type "C" Oil, Oil Daily
Saddle — Use Bed Way Lubricant, Oil Daily
Headstock Drain Plugs
Spindle Mount — Type "C" Oil, As Needed
Back Gear — Teflon Grease, Grease Monthly
Spindle Bearings — Type "A" Oil, Keep Full
Reverse Bracket — Type "C" Oil, Fill Daily
Twin Gears — Type "C" Oil, Oil Daily
Gear Box — Type "B" Oil, Fill Daily
Idler Gear — Type "C" Oil, Oil Daily
Tension Lever — Type "C" Oil, Oil Daily
Gear Reduction — Type "B" Oil, Keep Full, 16" Lathe
Sleeve Bearings — Type "A" Oil, Oil Monthly

Motor
Ball Bearings — Grease Every 2 Years If Fittings Are Present

Lubricating Oil Specifications
Machine Oil - Saybolt Universal Viscosity Rating in Seconds at 100° F

Type A:	Type B:	Type C:	Way:
100 Sec.	150-240 Sec.	250-500 Sec.	300-500 Sec.

Lubrication Chart
For 9" and 10K Lathes

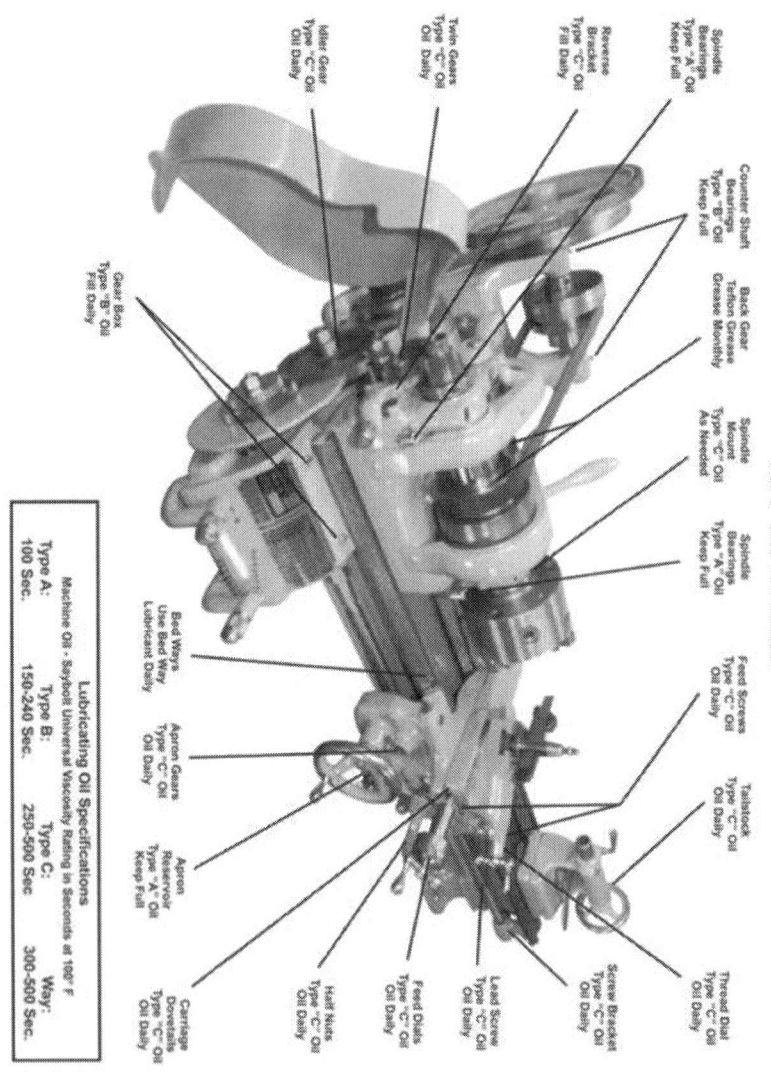

- Spindle Bearings — Type "A" Oil — Keep Full
- Reverse Bracket — Type "C" Oil — Fill Daily
- Twin Gears — Type "C" Oil — Oil Daily
- Miter Gear — Type "C" Oil — Oil Daily
- Counter Shaft Bearings — Type "B" Oil — Keep Full
- Gear Box — Type "B" Oil — Fill Daily
- Back Gear — Teflon Grease — Grease Monthly
- Spindle Mount — Type "C" Oil — As Needed
- Feed Screws — Type "C" Oil — Oil Daily
- Spindle Bearings — Type "A" Oil — Keep Full
- Bed Ways — Use Bed Way Lubricant Daily
- Apron Gears — Type "C" Oil — Oil Daily
- Apron Reservoir — Type "A" Oil — Keep Full
- Tailstock — Type "C" Oil — Oil Daily
- Thread Dial — Type "C" Oil — Oil Daily
- Screw Bracket — Type "C" Oil — Oil Daily
- Lead Screw — Type "C" Oil — Oil Daily
- Feed Dials — Type "C" Oil — Oil Daily
- Half Nuts — Type "C" Oil — Oil Daily
- Carriage Dovetails — Type "C" Oil — Oil Daily

Lubricating Oil Specifications
Machine Oil - Saybolt Universal Viscosity Rating in Seconds at 100° F
Type A: 100 Sec. Type B: 150-240 Sec. Type C: 250-500 Sec. Way: 300-500 Sec.

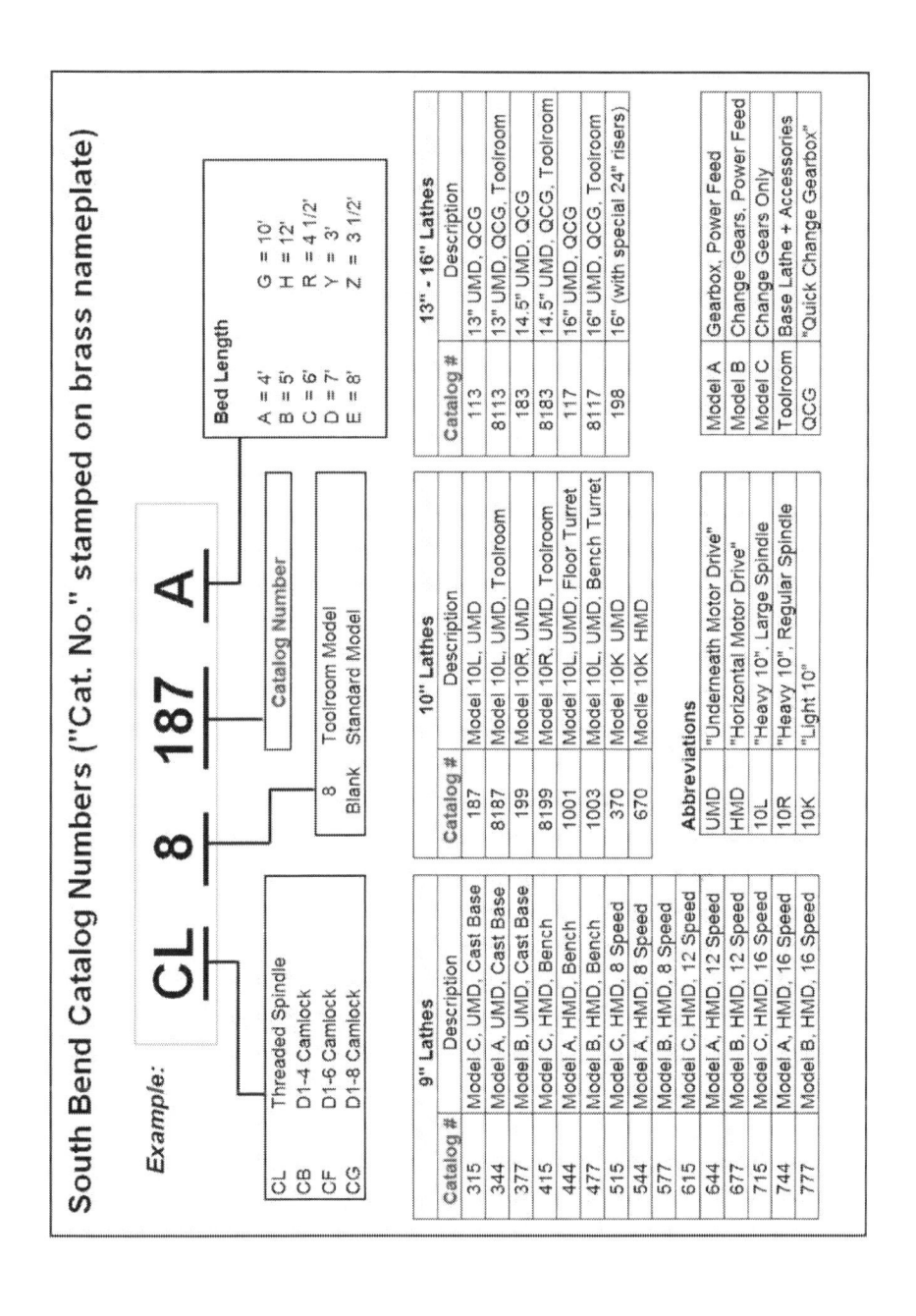

South Bend Catalog Numbers ("Cat. No." stamped on brass nameplate)

Example: **CL 8 187 A**

- CL → Threaded Spindle
- CB → D1-4 Camlock
- CF → D1-6 Camlock
- CG → D1-8 Camlock

- 8 → Toolroom Model
- Blank → Standard Model

Bed Length
- A = 4'
- B = 5'
- C = 6'
- D = 7'
- E = 8'
- G = 10'
- H = 12'
- R = 4 1/2'
- Y = 3'
- Z = 3 1/2'

9" Lathes

Catalog #	Description
315	Model C, UMD, Cast Base
344	Model A, UMD, Cast Base
377	Model B, UMD, Cast Base
415	Model C, HMD, Bench
444	Model A, HMD, Bench
477	Model B, HMD, Bench
515	Model C, HMD, 8 Speed
544	Model A, HMD, 8 Speed
577	Model B, HMD, 8 Speed
615	Model C, HMD, 12 Speed
644	Model A, HMD, 12 Speed
677	Model B, HMD, 12 Speed
715	Model C, HMD, 16 Speed
744	Model A, HMD, 16 Speed
777	Model B, HMD, 16 Speed

10" Lathes

Catalog #	Description
187	Model 10L, UMD
8187	Model 10L, UMD, Toolroom
199	Model 10R, UMD
8199	Model 10R, UMD, Toolroom
1001	Model 10L, UMD, Floor Turret
1003	Model 10L, UMD, Bench Turret
370	Model 10K UMD
670	Modle 10K HMD

13" - 16" Lathes

Catalog #	Description
113	13" UMD, QCG
8113	13" UMD, QCG, Toolroom
183	14.5" UMD, QCG
8183	14.5" UMD, QCG, Toolroom
117	16" UMD, QCG
8117	16" UMD, QCG, Toolroom
198	16" (with special 24" risers)

Abbreviations

UMD	"Underneath Motor Drive"
HMD	"Horizontal Motor Drive"
10L	"Heavy 10", Large Spindle
10R	"Heavy 10", Regular Spindle
10K	"Light 10"
Model A	Gearbox, Power Feed
Model B	Change Gears, Power Feed
Model C	Change Gears Only
Toolroom	Base Lathe + Accessories
QCG	"Quick Change Gearbox"

TOOLING DIMENSIONS

for SOUTH BEND LATHES

All dimensions are in inches and are subject to change

SWING OVER BED, SADDLE, COMPOUND REST

Size Lathe	9"	10 K	10"	13"	14 1/2"	16"
A	9 1/4	10	10 1/8	13 1/8	14 5/8	16 1/4
B	...	....	6 3/4	8 3/4	10 1/4	11 1/8
C	5 1/2	6 1/4	5 7/8	7 3/4	8 3/4	9 5/8

SPINDLE NOSE THREAD

Size Lathe	9" and 10 K	10" and 13" 1 1/8" Collet	13"-1 1/8" Collet	14 1/2"-3/4" Collet	14 1/2"-1 1/8" Collet	16"
E	1 1/2—8	2 1/4—8	1 7/8—8	2 1/4—6	2 3/8—6	2 3/8—6
F	11/16	15/16	1 1/8	1 5/16	1 3/8	1 3/8
G	1.509	2.259	1.884	2.259	2.384	2.384
H	7/8	1 3/16	1 3/8	1 5/8	1 3/4	1 3/4

SPINDLE TAPER, SPINDLE HOLE, SPINDLE LENGTH

Size Lathe	9"	10 K	10"-1 1/8" Collet	13"-1" Collet	13"-1 1/8" Collet	14 1/2"-3/4" Collet	14 1/2"-1 1/8" Collet	16"
B	.938	.938	1.629	1.231	1.629	1.325	1.629	1.629
D	.602	.602	.602	.623	.602	.602	.602	.602
K	49/64	53/64	1 13/32	1	1 13/32	1 1/8	1 13/32	1 13/32
N	2	2	2	3	3	3	3	3
J	12 1/4	12 1/4	13 23/32	19 3/16	21 1/16	22 31/64	24 29/64	24 11/16

TOOL POST OPENING

Size Lathe	9" and 10 K	10"	13"	14 1/2"	16"
D	19/32	19/32	1 3/64	1 7/32	1 7/32
M	13/32	15/32	19/32	21/32	23/32
N	7/8	....	1 1/4	1 3/4	1 3/4

COMPOUND REST TOP

Size Lathe	9" and 10 K	10"	13"	14 1/2"	16"
C	1 1/32	1 1/32	1 3/8	1 27/32	2 1/16
G	7/8	1	1 1/4	1 7/16	1 5/8
J	9/32	21/64	7/16	7/16	7/16
K	9/32	9/32	13/32	17/32	17/32
Y	2 1/2	2 7/8	3 3/8	4	4 1/2
W	1 9/32	1 13/32	1 49/64	2 1/64	2 17/64

COMPOUND REST BASE

Size Lathe	9"	10 K	10"	13"	14 1/2"	16"
O	2 5/8	2 5/8	2 7/8	4	4 1/8	4 5/8
P	3 5/16	3 5/16	3 5/16	4 1/2	5 1/8	5 3/4
Q	4 3/16	4 3/16	4 3/16	5 11/16	6 1/8	6 7/16
R	1 3/8	1 3/8	1 5/8	2 1/4	2 1/2	2 3/4
S	2 9/16	2 41/64	2 51/64	3 3/4	4 3/16	4 9/16

SADDLE DOVETAIL

Size Lathe	9"	10 K	10"	13"	14 1/2"	16"
A	3 19/32	3 43/64	3 61/64	5 7/32	5 3/4	6 3/16
B	.7655	.7655	.8328	1.1753	1.2690	1.4253
E	1.5253	1.5253	1.6032	2.1631	2.4756	2.7256
L	23/64	23/64	7/16	9/16	9/16	9/16
W	3 1/4	3 1/4	3 5/8	4 9/16	4 7/8	5 3/8
X	10 1/16	10 1/16	11 7/8	16 1/32	18 5/16	19 7/8

South Bend Lathe

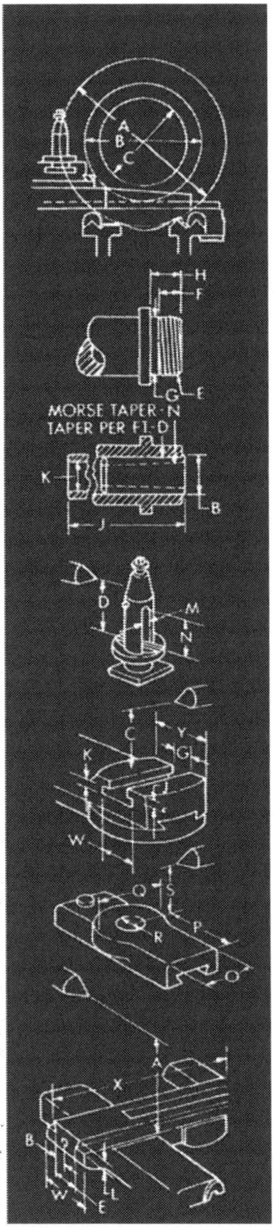

South Bend Lathe Approximate Serial Number Dates

Note that in late 1947, South Bend changed the lathe serial numbering format so that the serial number represents the quantity produced for each different lathe model. The letter suffix was unique to the model and there were additional letters after the suffix to denote other options (these letters are not included in the table). Roughly 350,000 lathes produced in total including minor variants not shown.

Year	Starting Serial Number	Year	Estimated Starting Serial Number					
			9"	10K	10"	13"	14.5"	16"
1910	700	1948	7,900N	500K	1,000R	500T	300F	600H
1911	1,000	1949	15,200N	1,000K	1,900R	1,000T	700F	1,700H
1912	1,150	1950	19,300N	1,500K	2,300R	1,600T	1,100F	2,900H
1913	2,000	1951	23,000N	2,200K	2,900R	2,200T	1,200F	3,500H
1914	3,000	1952	27,500N	2,500K	3,500R	2,900T	1,300F	4,300H
1915	4,000	1953	31,000N	2,900K	4,700R	3,300T	1,500F	5,500H
1916	6,000	1954	34,000N	3,300K	6,400R	3,900T	2,000F	6,600H
1917	11,850	1955	36,000N	3,800K	7,400R	4,600T	2,400F	7,200H
1918	15,600	1956	38,000N	4,500K	8,100R	5,300T	2,700F	8,100H
1919	19,500	1957	40,500N	5,400K	9,000R	6,100T	3,000F	9,000H
1920	21,800	1958	42,700N	5,700K	9,700R	6,700T	3,100F	9,300H
1921	23,300	1959	43,600N	7,000K	10,400R	7,100T	3,200F	9,600H
1922	24,800	1960	46,000N	7,400K	11,000R	7,600T	3,300F	10,000H
1923	28,000	1961	46,800N	7,600K	12,000R	8,100T	3,400F	10,400H
1924	30,000	1962	48,000N	9,000K	12,500R	9,100T	3,500F	10,800H
1925	31,000	1963	49,600N	9,500K	13,200R	9,500T	3,600F	11,200H
1926	32,000	1964	51,500N	10,200K	13,800R	9,800T	3,700F	11,600H
1927	33,500	1965	52,600N	10,800K	14,400R	10,200T	3,800F	12,000H
1928	37,300	1966	54,000N	11,800k	15,100R	10,700T	4,000F	12,400H
1929	41,000	1967	55,500N	12,700K	15,800R	11,200T		12,700H
1930	46,000	1968	56,800N	13,100K	16,500R	12,000T		12,800H
1931	47,900	1969	57,600N	13,800K	17,400R	12,700T		13,000H
1932	50,400	1970		14,800K	17,900R	13,100T		13,200H
1933	52,000	1971		18,000K	18,200R	13,600T		13,400H
1934	53,000	1972		22,000K	18,500R	13,800T		13,500H
1935	57,000	1973		31,000K	18,800R	14,200T		13,700H
1936	63,600	1974		31,800K	19,300R	14,400T		13,800H
1937	72,300	1975		32,500K	19,700R	14,600T		13,900H
1938	81,000	1976		33,500K	20,100R	15,100T		14,000H
1939	87,800	1977		34,300K	20,300R	15,500T		14,100H
1940	95,500	1978		34,900K	20,800R	15,800T		14,200H
1941	106,900	1979		35,300K	21,200R	16,100T		14,300H
1942	123,000	1980		36,500K	21,350R	16,400T		14,350H
1943	134,000	1981		37,800K	21,600R	16,600T		14,400H
1944	149,000	1982		39,000K	22,000R	16,800T		14,450H
1945	157,000	1983		40,300K	22,300R	16,900T		14,475H
1946	168,900	1984		40,600K	22,550R	17,000T		14,500H
1947	182,000	1985		41,000K	22,700R			14,525H
		1986		41,300K	22,750R			14,550H
		1987		41,600K	22,850R			14,600H
		1988		42,000K	22,950R			
		1989			23,000R			
		2002			23,200R			

Dates listed are the manufacturing date.

Resources for Vintage South Bend Lathe Owners

- **Additional Resources Available on the Internet:**

    www.practicalmachinist.com – A great South Bend Lathe forum for owners and machinists.

    www.wswells.com - A site dedicated to South Bend Lathes, literature, catalogs and a database of surviving lathes.

    www.VintageMachinery.org – A great resource for documents and other vintage reading materials.

- **Lathe Parts (New and Used):**

    South Bend Lathe Co.: www.southbendlathe.com (Successor to the original South Bend Lathe)

    Ebay: www.ebay.com – Business and Industrial Section - Metalworking

- **Lathe Rebuild Kits, Manuals & Special Tools:**

Parts Kits, specialty tools, manuals, felt wipers, gaskets, and lubricants for rebuilding most models of vintage South Bend Lathes.

Shopping On-Line

Ebay: http://stores.ebay.com/stevewb
Amazon: search " ILION Industrial "

Snail Mail:

ILION Industrial Services, LLC
PO Box 80502
Raleigh, NC 27623-0502
email: ilion@bellsouth.net

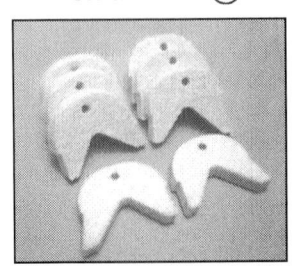

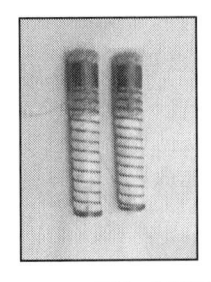